Project Gotham Racing 2

Prima's Official Strategy Guide

Jon Dudlak

Prima Games
A Division of Random House, Inc.

3000 Lava Ridge Court
Roseville, CA 95661
1-800-733-3000
www.primagames.com

ISBN: 0-7615-4345-7
Library of Congress Catalog Card Number: 2003110275
Printed in the United States of America

03 04 05 06 GG 10 9 8 7 6 5 4 3 2 1

CONTENTS

INTRODUCTION

Success in *Project Gotham Racing 2* depends not just on how you place in a race, but how you drive getting to the finish line. This strategy guide is designed to help you perform better in both areas by presenting a track-by-track walkthrough of the Kudos World Series mode. While *Project Gotham Racing 2* offers several different gameplay modes, the Kudos World Series is the heart of the single-player game. The driving tips you learn here can be applied to Arcade Racing, Xbox *Live*, or any other challenge, because they all use the same courses.

Each individual track breakdown in this guide is based on the Expert difficulty level. Expert level is both the most difficult and most rewarding level of play. Some will take dozens of attempts to conquer, but the payoff in Kudos is usually worth the effort. For those players choosing Hard or Medium difficulty, these driving concepts and tips still apply, but the requirements aren't as stringent nor the competition as fierce. After all, if you can master the Expert challenges, you can drive anywhere!

DRIVER'S ED

This section will help you learn how to drive efficiently in *PGR 2*.

Steering

Because the shortest distance between two points is a straight line, avoid unnecessary directional changes. Look for a path through broader curves that minimizes steering. Turning creates additional friction and weight-distribution changes that can slow your car down, or worse, spin it out. Every fraction of a second counts in a race, so master your driving lines and you'll see a marked improvement in your times.

Drifting

Drifting is the most important concept to learn for dealing with the various turns you'll encounter in *Project Gotham Racing 2*. Drifting refers to the amount of lateral movement your car undergoes as a result of centripetal forces. Essentially, it's how much the car tends to "slide" away from your normal driving line as you make a turn. You control this phenomenon by using the steering wheel, accelerator, and brake to make the car behave a certain way. Master the following four types of controlled drifting and learn when to use each one.

Standard Drifting

Standard drifting involves no special accelerator or brake work, and the back tires stay planted on the asphalt. Accomplish it by simply steering through a turn and letting the car's inertia carry it to the outside of the track. This type of drifting is the most desirable because it has a relatively low impact on your speed and direction. Standard drifting requires either a low curve-entry speed or broad track to accomplish, so it is the least versatile controlled-drifting method.

Passive Drifting

To drift passively, let off the accelerator just before you enter the turn, stay off the gas while steering, then accelerate out once you're clear. This affords you a tighter turning radius than accelerating through the curve and gets you through the moderately wide turns without breaking your traction. On tighter turns, use this method to break your rear-wheel grip and kick the back end out a little for a controlled slide. The game refers to this as a "slide," and you get a Kudos bonus any time you do one. Simply take the turn a little tighter and cut the wheel more sharply to achieve this effect.

Power Drifting

Also called "power sliding," this method is similar to passive drifting through tighter turns but uses the accelerator to break the rear-tire traction. Let off the gas before you enter the curve. Just after you begin your turn, accelerate hard to spin the back wheels and drive the back end of the car outward. Once the car is pointing the right direction to exit the curve, meter your gas-pedal pressure to regain control of the back end. Since this method relies on breaking traction of the driven tires, you won't be able to power drift with front-wheel-drive cars. The weight distribution keeps the powered wheels glued to the ground on these cars, so pay attention to your chosen car's drivetrain setup.

Brake Drifting

Brake drifting can be done using either the brake pedal or handbrake. As you enter a turn, hit the brakes hard and your rear end will swing out immediately. The handbrake will give you a sudden "kick" from the back end, while the brake pedal yields more of a controlled slide. Mastering use of both methods is the key to earning extra Kudos and surviving the Expert-level Timed Lap and Hot Lap challenges later in the game, where you will be required to make very tight laps.

Braking

Good braking technique can be just as important as quick acceleration. Learning to accept that you *have* to slow down sometimes to drive well is an important first step. Feathering the brake when entering a turn settles your car gently to a more manageable speed and conserves your energy when exiting.

Braking hard puts you into a harsh slide that can be either useful or detrimental in different situations. Learn which turns need to be taken which way to maximize your score and minimize lap times.

Controlled Contact

Because you don't get penalized for running into other cars (apart from a potential loss of speed), use fellow racers as tools for helping you around difficult corners. By using another car as a crutch to keep yourself stable, you often can overtake aggressive leaders. Plowing into a rival while skidding sideways on the inside of the track is often very useful. You also can ram him from behind to throw him off course and keep yourself pointed in the right direction.

Drafting

Wind resistance can be a huge drag when you're trying to build speed, especially if your car isn't terribly aerodynamic. But if you can drive directly in line behind another car on the track, you pick up an extra boost by using it as a windblock. This technique is called "drafting." Just slip in behind one of your rivals and follow (the faster you're going, the farther back you should be). You soon begin to overtake him, so jog out to the side and use your windless momentum to pass.

The racing line is an "outside-inside-outside" path through a turn that will earn you bonus Kudos and keep your time trimmed down. Enter the turn on the far outside and cut in close across the inside corner (follow the skid marks in the pavement). You will drift outward a little upon exit and end up near the outside wall. Watch the computer's cars race; they almost always use this method to negotiate turns.

THE KUDOS SYSTEM

The single-player World Tour is all about driving well enough to earn Kudos, which are used to get your hands on better, faster cars. Kudos are earned in a variety of ways:

Race Completion Bonus

At the end of every race in each series, you are awarded a Kudos completion bonus based on the difficulty of the challenge. It might be anywhere from a couple hundred Kudos for a Novice challenge to several thousand Kudos in an Expert mode.

Every time you complete a challenge, the total number of Kudos you earned during the race is combined with your completion bonus to yield a final number. If you've completed the challenge before on any difficulty level, your previous Kudos earnings are subtracted from this total, thus only your newly earned Kudos count toward your score. So you can't go back and replay races to rack up Kudos, but you can try to better your last score and make a few extra Kudos. After each race, the Kudos you've earned will be displayed in the Kudos breakdown screen.

Earned In Game Kudos

There are several ways to accumulate Kudos. Your good driving techniques can win you Kudos for the following:

Clean Section: 25 Kudos. Make it through a defined section of the track without hitting a wall.

Nice Slide: Kudos awarded varies with degree of slide and duration. Break traction with the back tires and skid through a turn

Good Line: Kudos award varies with speed and path. Take a corner or contour in the road cleanly at good speed.

"360": Kudos award varies with speed and originality. Spin the car all the way around. You get an initial Kudos bonus and a significantly smaller one with every subsequent spin until the game just stops rewarding you. It's not very practical for most races, but sometimes it's just fun to make a huge doughnut on Lower Wacker Drive.

Sweet Overtake: 50 Kudos. Overtake another car on the track. You'll earn a smaller reward each time you overtake a previously passed car.

Position Bonus: 200 points for first place, 100 for second, and 50 if you come in third.

Drafting: Point award varies with duration. Use a car in front to block your wind and up your speed. Turn it into an easy combo by drafting into an overtake, or alternating drafting between different cars.

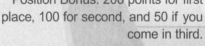

Kudos Rank Levels

The following are the first 50 levels of Kudos Token awards issued to the player upon reaching the corresponding Kudos levels:

RANK	Kudos	TOKENS AWARDED
1	0	0
2	4,000	2
3	8,750	2
4	14,000	3
5	20,250	3
6	27,000	4
7	34,500	4
8	42,500	5
9	51,500	5
10	61,000	6
11	71,250	6
12	82,000	7
13	93,750	7
14	106,000	8
15	119,000	8
16	132,750	9
17	147,000	10
18	162,000	10
19	178,000	10
20	194,250	15
21	211,500	15
22	229,250	15
23	247,750	15
24	267,000	15
25	286,250	15
26	305,500	15
27	324,750	15
28	344,000	15
29	363,250	15
30	382,500	15
31	401,750	17
32	421,000	17
33	440,250	17
34	459,500	17
35	478,750	17
36	498,000	17
37	517,250	18
38	536,500	18
39	555,750	18
40	575,000	20
41	613,000	20
42	670,000	20
43	745,750	20
44	840,250	20
45	953,500	20
46	1,066,750	20
47	1,180,000	20
48	1,293,500	20
49	1,406,750	20
50	1,520,000	20

Fastest Lap: 100 Kudos. Get the lowest lap time for the course.

Clean Race: 250 Kudos. Complete the course without hitting any walls significantly.

Two Wheels: Kudos award varies with time in air. Kick your two front, rear, or side wheels up into the air by hitting a bump or curb.

Cool Air: Kudos award varies with time in air. Get all four wheels off the ground by hitting a bump or hill at high speed.

The best and fastest way to build a mountain of Kudos is to string your tricks into a big combo. After you perform any Kudos-earning technique, you have two seconds to connect it with another and begin a combo. As long as you keep this pacing up, you earn a base amount plus a bonus that builds with every new trick. The Cone Challenge stages are built around this combo-building technique, so get very familiar with it on these levels.

COMPACT SPORTS SERIES

The Compact Sports series consists of seven challenges built for small, typically four-cylinder sports cars.

Recommended Cars:
Seat Leon Cupra R

This car can be used to complete almost the entire series, so the walkthrough here shows you how to do use the Leon to its fullest until you can afford to buy the Ford Focus RS.

Ford Focus RS

Make this the one car you buy for this series. It vastly outperforms any of the other offerings and is a must-have if you want to beat the final Street Race on Expert level. If you ever get stuck using the Leon, just bring out the Focus and you'll see vast improvement.

Street Race 1

Track: Duomo 2, Florence
Car: Seat Leon Cupra R

Hit the gas hard off the line and overtake the third-place MINI before the first turn.

Stay on the accelerator and take the second and third bends as close as you can to the inside guardrail. This should land you a second-place position, as the computer takes these turns wide with the leading cars.

Now for the Beetle. He slows to take the next turn on the outside, so cut inside and step in front of him. Kick your back tires out and slide into him if need be; you don't get penalized Kudos for ramming him, and it helps slow him down.

With the competition behind, you've got a clear look at the rest of the track. Stay to the right on the straight-away and cut hard to the inside of the next turn to set yourself up on the left side.

Power slide through the right-hand turn that immediately follows, then accelerate straight through the offset in the track. Get to the right for the next curve.

Just before the curve begins, let off the gas and cut in hard to the left. Remain turned to the left as you ease on and off the accelerator for the rest of this long turn, drifting from the track's center at the start to the far right by the end. If you do it right, you won't have to brake at all.

The finish line is just ahead. One more lap and the race is yours.

One on One

Track: Duomo 1, Florence
Car: Seat Leon Cupra R

The straightaway leads to a wide turn, so take it tight on the inside and don't slow down. There's plenty of drifting room on the opposite side. Check your rearview mirror periodically to make sure that speedy Lancia isn't gaining on you.

You start this race slightly behind your rival, so overtaking is your immediate concern. Follow his path around the gradual bend ahead of the starting line, then jog just left of him as you follow into the second turn.

Your opponent invariably brakes to make this directional change. Use this opportunity to sneak in close to the inside curb, and brake hard to kick out the back and graze his driver's side. This messes up his line and spins him out if you can clip his rear, but even a sideways push buys you enough space to sneak ahead.

Start braking early to slide through this next turn or you'll end up against the outside guardrail once you get through it. Start accelerating again as soon as you're past the corner and pointed toward the track's center.

If your speed is suffering a little from the collision, take the following right turn wide and accelerate through. Otherwise, you have to kick the back out and drift to avoid hitting the opposite wall of buildings.

This last turn can make or break the race, so hit it without crashing or spinning out. Start wide and cut in as close as you can to the inside guardrail. Let off the accelerator to get a tighter turn, and brake if you have to. Even if you lose a little speed here, you can cross the line in first place as long as you take the turn cleanly.

Cone Challenge

Track: Under the Bridge, Sydney
Car: Ford Focus RS

Start out strong and accelerate through the first eight cone gates without braking. Get a good, broad line between the third and fourth gate so you don't hit the wall and lose your combo.

Let off the gas as you approach the ninth gate (it's okay to brake a little here) and slide gently through so you can cut hard across the track to the right. The 10th gate is on this side. Do a recovery slide to make this tight turn through the gate and right yourself at the same time.

The key to mastering the Expert Cone Challenges lies in chaining combos throughout the track in a clean race.

One on One
Track: Dawes Point Loop, Sydney
Car: Ford Focus RS

On this next turn, slide to keep your combo going. Swing wide to the left and brake to skid across and through the 11th gate.

Start by getting directly behind your rival's VW Golf R32 and follow to the first turn.

Use the next straightaway to build speed and keep your combo going through cone gates and clean section bonuses at the painted lines. You've got one more tough turn with a skid at gate 17, but make it through and you're home free. If you kept the combo going, you should finish just clear of the required minimum.

As he swings out to make this tight turn, brake a little and cut to the inside. If you swing out too far, the worst you do is run into your opponent and right yourself. Now you have the inside lane and can cross the second part of this turn into the lead.

Check your rearview to make sure the Golf isn't drafting behind you as you hit the straightaway. Maintain enough speed to pull a two-wheel jump at the painted lines here for an easy combo (provided your previous section was clean). Stay right and take the upcoming turn tight by drifting across the inside.

The next turn to be wary of is the track's northernmost point. If you're doing 70 or so, power drift or brake drift a little to keep from hitting the opposite girder.

For the last bend, set up on the far left and power through the turn at full speed. It's wide enough that you don't need to slow down here to keep from crashing, and the finish line is just ahead. If your opponent gets ahead of you into the second lap here, just stay close. The straightaway is a great place to drift on him and overtake.

Street Race 2

Track: Gamla Stan Loop, Stockholm
Car: Seat Leon Cupra R

Get behind the third-place Civic and start drafting when you're up to speed. Don't draft the Lancia that's slightly ahead or the Civic will come from behind and spin you out. Keep this up until the first turn is in sight.

With all four cars matching speed and going into this turn, it's kind of a crapshoot as to what might happen. Take the inside and use your buddies as a cushion– just be careful not to scrape the guardrail if you're trying to maximize your Kudos. You come out of the turn in a very narrow first place.

Make sure no one's on your tail as you head into the straightaway. A collision here can really mess you up. Follow the tire marks on the street to line up your next turn. End up on the right side after it's done.

Speed Camera

Track: Speed Camera
Track 1, Stockholm
Car: Ford Focus RS

Choose the Ford Focus RS to make this quick race easy on yourself. It's possible with the Leon, but if you have the Focus, don't waste your time with anything else. You need to clear 93 mph in order to make the grade here.

You can take the gradual bends heading toward the hairpin at full speed, but drift through the first sharp turn and stay to the right before you hit the 180-degree hairpin. If you slow down too much, though, you'll surely get passed here.

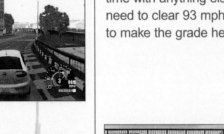

Take off from the starting line and get to the left to follow the tire treads in the street. Stick to this path for the best angle on these corners. Work up to about 60 mph—you don't need a ton of speed here yet.

Get through this hairpin and take the remaining mild turn left at top speed to make up for any previous loss in velocity. The starting gate lies just ahead.

You'll drift wide a little after the first turn, so get over to the right side to make the second at around 50 mph. Stay in line with the tire marks and cut tight to the inside (left) of the second curve.

When you've recovered from the second bend, get to the left and make sure you're on the gas hard before you start your final turn to clear the level at 93 mph.

Fortunately, once you have the lead, this track is pretty forgiving. The Focus chases all the way to the end, so stay sharp and watch your back. You don't have to drop speed until you make the westernmost turn on the track to head north. Make this without braking by power sliding.

Street Race 3

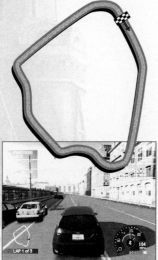

Track: Gamla Oval, Stockholm
Car: Ford Focus RS

To snatch first place, you need the Focus RS here. Start out by overtaking the fifth-place Civic and drafting behind the fourth-place VW R32. Build some speed until you can overtake the VW and the Lancia. This puts you right behind the lead cars, a Focus and a Renault Clio V6.

Same goes for the final turn. Drift onto the shoulder when you come out of the turn and don't lose too much speed. You've got two more laps—run them strongly but conservatively through the turns to finish the Compact Sports series.

If you're lucky, these lead cars will get tangled up trying to make the turn and you'll get an easy shot at first place by passing on the inside. Otherwise, you have to catch them after the turn, which is less desirable, but doable. The Renault Clio V6 can't match your speed, but the leading Focus is a beast to catch. Draft off his back and scoot around him.

SPORTS CONVERTIBLE SERIES

Seven challenges define the Sports Convertible series. Cars in this set of races tend to have better power and handling than those of the Compact Sports class.

Recommended Cars:
Porsche Boxster
The Boxster is the fastest and best overall car for the course, if you can afford it. Its excellent top speed makes it the go-to vehicle for any Expert-level challenge.

Honda S2000
A very capable substitute for the Boxster, the S2000 will save you one Kudos token if you want to be a cheapskate. Anything it can do the Boxster can do, though, so the game plan is the same for both cars.

Overtake
Track: Kremlin 1, Moscow
Car: Honda S2000

This Expert trial requires you to overtake the first-place car (you must overtake four cars) within four minutes. Complete laps on the loop-shaped track at maximum speed until you can lap these guys. Check your pacing against the following timetable to see if you're on schedule for a win. Our recommended pacing leaves about five seconds on the clock after safely passing the final car, so if you're ahead of these times, you're in good shape.

Car #6: Lap 2, 3:13 remaining

Car #7: Lap 1, 3:40 remaining

Car #5: Lap 2, 3:02 remaining

Car #4: Lap 3, 2:22 remaining

Car #3: Lap 4, 1:37 remaining

Car #2: Lap 4, 1:27 remaining

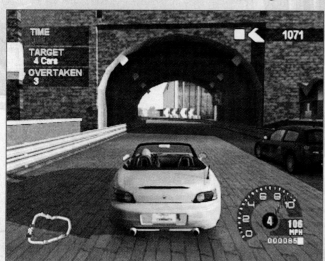

Car #1: Lap 7, :05 remaining

Street Race 1

Track: St. Basil's Circle, Moscow
Car: Honda S2000

You're not up against tough cars here, so this one's an easy score. Take an early lead by passing the second- and third-place cars in the straightaway. Pass the lead car in the first turn by taking the inside lane.

Be aware of the jump just before the dual arches. Remain pointed toward the left-hand arch for a wider reach on the opposite turn.

The road jogs ahead but don't slow down. Your competition doesn't falter, so don't get left behind for being too cautious.

Slow down for the sharp turn at the track's northern tip or you'll end up in the wall. Take the curve that follows at full speed, but set up for one more jog in the track as you exit. Keep to the right lane for a good line. The finish is just ahead.

Street Race 2

Track: Piazza della Repubblica, Florence
Car: Honda S2000

To get the early lead, step on the gas through the first two turns and take them hard to the inside. There's just enough room to squeeze between the wall and the Toyota in the first turn, and the Honda in the second turn.

Brake lightly in the next turn, and cut in close to the wall for a good line. The next bend, in the southeast corner, is gradual enough to take without dropping your speed.

The last turn requires light braking to navigate. Check your rearview to make sure the Honda isn't trying to slide past.

One on One

Track: Uffizi, Florence
Car: Honda S2000

This time you're going head-to-head with another a Boxster. He starts ahead, so follow his lead into the narrow straightaway and draft if you can.

At the end, brake and drift to negotiate an awkward left turn. Use this opportunity to slip by your rival and into the lead.

Set up on the left to take the next right turn. Follow the tire marks close to the right rail for the best line, using the broad space on the left to recover.

The next part of this track contains a few choice segments from other Florence courses, so it will seem familiar. Remember the tight turn on the far-eastern edge and the long bend that follows. This leads to a very wide turn through an archway—take it at top speed.

Two cramped turns between you and the finish line are visible on the map's west side. Slow down to make these. If you've got the lead here, use the narrow alley walls to block your opponent from passing.

Cone Challenge

Track: Lenin, Moscow
Car: Honda S2000

To score the whopping 13,725 Kudos needed to pass the Expert Cone Challenge, you have to combo through the entire level. This will take several tries, so don't get discouraged. Gun it through the first five gates to build speed. For the sixth gate, kick the back out and slide to keep the combo going. Don't touch the cones as you glide through this or any other cone gate. If you lose your combo at any time, start over.

Keep the gas floored all the way to the next major curve, making sure you hit every cone gate (and clean section bonus) along the way to keep your combo going.

Slide through the gate at the end of the next curve to maintain speed. If you slow down too much, you won't be able to combo the next few cone gates.

On the next turn, power slide through the cone gate and across the white line that marks the section split. A clean section bonus here continues your combo until the next cone gate section.

Stand on the gas through the straightaway so you don't lose the Kudos combo. Even as you slide through the cone gate at the final turn, be sure your speed doesn't drop below 50 coming out of the skid; these last cone gate segments are pretty far apart.

Stay in control as you pick up the cone gate that's offset to the left. Throw in one more slide across the finish line to add some last-second Kudos. With the Clean Race bonus of 250 Kudos, you should clear 4,300. If you fall a few Kudos short, redo the course, trying to extend your power slides to eke out a few more Kudos this time.

When the inside track girder disappears from view, accelerate out of the turn and steer hard to the right. Straighten out and make only light steering taps to navigate the contours of the track ahead. Keep the gas pressed hard and you should clear the 106 mph mark by the time the camera goes off.

Speed Camera

Track: Speed Camera 1, Moscow
Car: Porsche Boxster

Street Race 3

Track: Red Square 2, Moscow
Car: Honda S2000

Get in line to draft the BMW. This allows you to pass the MR2 on the left. When you're past the Toyota, edge out to the right and accelerate hard toward the turn.

Accelerate down the first half of the horseshoe-shaped track to about 60 mph. Enter the curve on the left side so you can make a tight turn on the inside of the bend ahead, maintaining your speed.

Stay inside and slow down to make this sharp turn. Don't drift too much, and aim to get in line behind the Honda (following the first-place Boxster). Stay as close to this guy's tail as you can.

You can squeak by the Honda if you made the turn without losing too much velocity, but don't worry if you fall behind. Stay to the center-right for the next turn and take it tight on the inside without braking. The key to catching the Porsche is making the next few turns flawlessly.

Watch the jump in the road; it's parallel to the front of the large red building on the right. Take it at full speed, but point toward the center of the track before launching so you don't crash upon landing. Cut the next two turns lean on the inside so you don't have to brake.

Run hard until just before the next turn. Brake lightly and follow the tire marks that lead toward the hard bend ahead. Feather the brake through the turn and accelerate on the way out. You might be able to overtake the Porsche here, but don't become over-eager–you might wind up in a crash.

Drive cleanly and keep the pressure on the Porsche's tail–you'll catch him before long. Draft to gain a little speed, and look for a chance to pass. Turns work best because you can lean on him a little as you edge past.

COUPE SERIES

Now that you've gotten your feet wet, it's time to test your skills on some new types of trials with speedier cars. The Coupe series tacks on one additional challenge for a total of eight.

Recommended Cars:
Mazda RX-8 (Starter)
It's loose in the corners and not terribly fast, but the RX-8 will get you started in the speed trials. You can use the Integra for lower-speed tracks that require better handling.

BMW M3
You need to pick this car up to complete the overtake challenge here. Its top speed will help with longer races.

Audi S4
If you have the tokens to spare, this is the most drivable car of the lot. It's comparable to the BMW, but a little slower overall. Make the S4 your daily driver, and pull out the M3 if it fails you.

The Timed Run, you must beat the clock (shown in the screen's upper-right) to the finish. Fortunately, this track is familiar--it's the same one as in the second One on One challenge in the Compact Sports series. Refer to that section's strategy for track navigation. You need to rein in the powerful S4 a little around the turns; compensate to maintain control.

Timed Run
Track: Dawes Point Loop, Sydney
Car: Audi S4

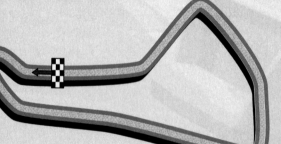

PGR 2

Street Race 1

Track: Cumberland Street, Sydney
Car: Audi S4

The northern point is a hairpin turn. Start braking early and get a good spin around the inside wall, then fade out to the right as you come off the turn.

Speed Camera

Track: Speed Camera Track 1, Sydney
Car: BMW M3

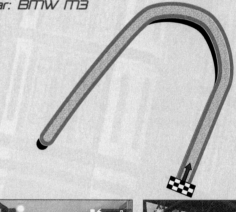

Slip easily through the pack and get up close behind the two lead cars. Set up inside and brake drift to cause a jam-up in the turn. You come out ahead if you do it right.

Accelerate to 70 mph and hug the track's right side. Make your turn across the middle and keep accelerating.

Stay to the left and cut right across the next turn at full speed. Stay right for the next turn, which you must slow down slightly to make. Afterward, you've got a nice clear stretch up the east side.

You get very close to the right wall but shouldn't touch. Pull left to cut across the inner point of the last bend, then accelerate out. You should be at a minimum of 80 mph.

You nearly graze the right wall as you pull out of this curve under full gas. Gently straighten out and finish at 105 mph.

One on One

Track: Harbour Bridge, Sydney
Car: Audi S4

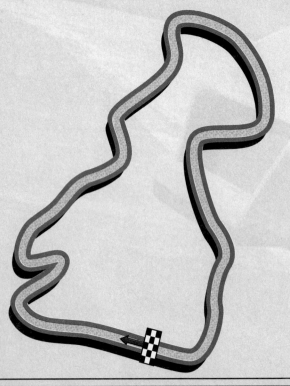

Pull up next to your opponent's Audi and remain just touching his left side as you approach the first turn. Just before he begins to make his cut across, apply pressure to his rear quarter-panel with your nose. You're pointed in the right direction for the turn as he veers off into the wall. This buys you a few seconds as the leader.

Take the next turn cautiously as it's on a slight downhill slope. Brake to about 30 mph to make it safely. Take the following turn wide at 50 mph as you regain speed.

Don't slow down for the mild S-curve ahead, but be prepared to fade right where the lanes split. Don't come off too hot when the lanes re-merge or you'll nail the back wall. Slow to about 60.

PGR 2

The remainder of the track is broad, so keep your speed up and don't make abrupt steering changes. Take the final corner bend from the left and swiftly cut across to keep your good line.

Cone Challenge

Track: Northern 2, Stockholm
Car: Audi S4

It takes real dedication to master this Cone Challenge on the Expert level. You need to attain 15,000 Kudos in two laps, which amounts to one big combo. Here are a few tips to get you there:

Slide to get Kudos bonuses between cone gates. This keeps your Kudos combo from dying out.

Heading into the alley in the track's northeastern section, let off the gas at the last cone gate, before entering the narrow passage (right before the stripes in the pavement). Coast into the next gate in time, then brake to make the tight corner gate and still keep your combo.

Make sure you get as many Good Line bonuses as you can. These keep your combo going in sections where cone gates are too far apart to reach in time.

This is a two-lap course, so you have a lot of ground to cover. You can't combo in the very first cone gate, but you can on the second lap. The starting line gives you a clean section bonus to carry your combo over to the second lap, provided you didn't crash at the end of the first one.

Car #6: Lap 1, 3:01 remaining

Car #5: Lap 1, 2:43 remaining

Even the slightest nick on a marker cone can cause you to lose your Kudos combo. Plus, a whacked cone can destroy a cone gate you might need to hit on the second lap. If the red K of doom shows up in the corner, reset and try again.

Car #4: Lap 2, 2:03 remaining

Car #3: Lap 2, 1:30 remaining

Overtake

Track: Gamla Island Hopping, Stockholm
Car: BMW M3

The only real tricky part of the race is the first turn. Take it tight on the inside and don't skid too much—it will cost you plenty of time. Your overtake schedule should look something like this:

Car #2: Lap 3, :25 remaining

Car #1: Lap 4, :02 remaining

Car #7: Lap 1, 3:41 remaining

Hot Lap

Track: Round the Riksdagshuset, Stockholm
Car: Audi S4

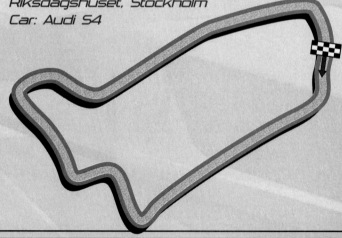

The Hot Lap begins with a rolling start. Jam on the gas to keep the car going before you cross the start line. Cut as close as you can across the right-hand girder for a good line.

At the end of the straightaway, drop your speed to make the sharp, narrow turn in the alleyway. You can make it around at about 40 mph.

The S-curve that follows is narrow, so work both sides of the track: Start on the left entering the first segment and drift right out of the first turn. Take the second curve on the right side and after the turn use the extra space on the left for drifting.

Take the two quick turns on the map's western edge a little slower than cruising speed; shoot for around 50 mph.

You're in the clear to stay on the gas for a while, but get ready to slow down when you start seeing the yellow "100m" curve signs on the left side of the road. The final turn requires another drop to 50 mph.

Street Race 2

Track: Island Hop, Stockholm
Car: Audi S4

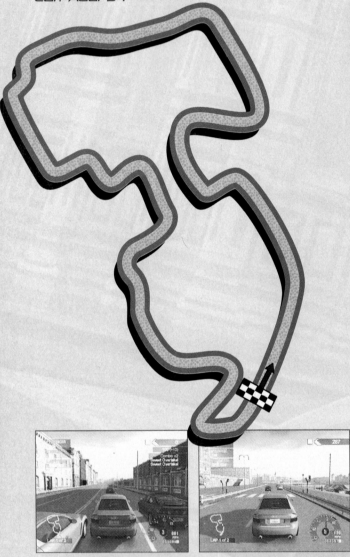

Now make your move. Go into this turn anticipating a lot of colliding with the lead three cars. When they start to brake, power through and knock slowing cars aside. You have to battle into the second turn, but persist and you emerge ahead in the straightaway.

The first rule of *Project Gotham Racing 2* is that an object in the lead tends to stay in the lead. So take the lead as soon as you can, and don't let anyone by! Start by breaking through the pack into a solid fourth-place position before the first hard turn.

Protect your lead. Be conservative through the turns. Slow down if that guarantees control. And take advantage of the S4's speed in the straightaways—you can clear 100 mph in the longer ones.

One more tricky turn lies just before the end of the track. You've seen it before in the previous series—it's a tight hairpin that empties into a wide stretch. Hug the inside at a controlled speed and drift wide into the space ahead. The finish line is just around the next turn.

An S-curve at the top of this track doesn't really show up on the overhead map. It comes up fast, so prepare to take it down around 40 mph.

SPORT UTILITY SERIES

The eight challenges here range from easy to mildly frustrating.

Recommended Cars:
Chevrolet SSR
Ditch this car as soon as humanly possible and buy the Porsche Cayenne Turbo. It makes your life so much better.

Porsche Cayenne Turbo
The only place this Sports Utility Vehicle has trouble is in the Expert time trial (Hot Lap). It doesn't corner terribly well, but the Porsche makes all the other events manageable.

Hot Lap
Track: Princes Street East, Edinburgh
Car: Porsche Cayenne

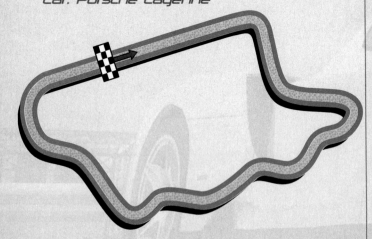

You have to go all out on this track to make the 58-second time requirement. If you screw up, it's all over. Start strong and line up on the left to take a clean turn just inside the girder. Get to the right to make the next couple of turns. Slow down just a little by keeping the accelerator pressed hard and feathering the brake.

Cut every corner you can and make sure your slides don't slow you down. Don't stop even if you scrape the wall a little or even lose a combo bonus as long as you're making good time. Even if you take one turn somewhat poorly, you can make up the time if you ace a later one.

Go as hard as you can through the mild curves in the middle of the track. Don't let off the gas for even a second until you need to slow down for the turn at the end. If you come out of the final turn with about 50 seconds on the clock, you should make it to the finish just in time.

Speed Camera
Track: Speed Camera Track 1, Edinburgh
Car: Porsche Cayenne

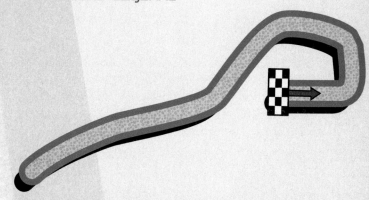

Despite the rain, the Cayenne has enough traction to get you through this trial at the exact requirement: 115 mph. Don't worry about building speed until after the first sharp turn. Start from 20-30 mph and hug the right wall as you accelerate.

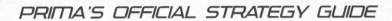

You end up scraping the back wall just a touch if you hug the second turn on the inside and drift outward. It's okay as long as you don't hit it too hard. Continue accelerating and cut across into the final stretch.

Keep standing on the gas as you navigate the last few hundred feet, making only light taps on the pad to steer. You should just clear 115 mph as you hit the finish line.

Street Race 1
Track: Princes Street loop, Edinburgh
Car: Porsche Cayenne

This race is in the bag if you drive the Porsche well. You out-accelerate the pack off the line and reach third place by the time you hit the first turn. Use any leaders for support and lean into them to jockey for position. You may get passed, but not by anyone you can't overtake very soon.

Use the Cayenne's unmatched acceleration to make some space behind you in the straightaway. This gives you a chance to pass any more hangers-on. Slow quickly before the turn and make it comfortably. Use the whole lane and stay toward the center so others can't pass by.

One more corner leads to another straightaway dotted with a couple of mild jogs in the track. Don't slow down for these unless you're well over 100 miles per hour.

The three tight turns at the end of the track are the only real advantage Kudos for nimble opponents. Your handling is a little poorer than most, so use your bulk to guard the lane. Check the rearview periodically to secure your lead.

Don't slow down until you approach that sharp bend in the northwest corner. Slow to about 25 mph and take it slowly. If you nail the back wall head-on, your rival will catch you and overtake as you struggle to get free.

One on One

Track: Grassmarket Eight, Edinburgh
Car: Porsche Cayenne

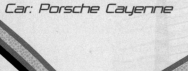

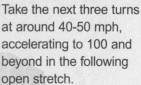

Take the next three turns at around 40-50 mph, accelerating to 100 and beyond in the following open stretch.

Prepare to embarrass your opponent. This track has both turns and long straightaways. And while your rivals can keep up in the turns, you leave him way behind when you hit the clearings. Start by overtaking and gliding downhill into the first straight run.

The next turnaround isn't nearly as sharp as the first. It's broken up by a short stretch of straight road, so regain a little speed here. Just be careful of the left turn that slopes downhill. Slow to about 20 mph to make it before taking off for the finish.

Cone Challenge

Track: Arno 2, Florence
Car: Porsche Cayenne

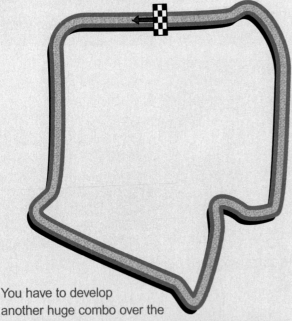

You have to develop another huge combo over the two laps of this course to meet the 13,000-Kudos goal. The Porsche is up to the task, but it's still an SUV that doesn't quite have the cornering and slide potential of your two-seaters. Here are a couple of spots you should watch out for as you chain the cone gates together to net the big score:

At the map's very bottom corner is a tight turn. If you have to slow down and almost stop, try to sneak in a slide before doing so to give yourself a chance to combo in the gate following the turn.

You also need to slide to link corner turns with lots of space between cone gates. You lose some velocity on the corner as it is, so don't let the slide bring you to a stop or you might not have enough speed left to pick up the next couple of gates in time.

Overtake

Track: Duomo 1, Florence
Car: Porsche Cayenne

Use the Porsche and maintain a steady speed throughout this track. Keep off the narrow Florence walls and this is what your times will look like:

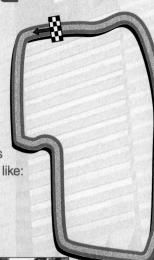

Car #7: Lap 1, 2:48 remaining

Car #6: Lap 1, 2:26 remaining

Car #5: Lap 2, 1:47 remaining

Car #4: Lap 3, 1:29 remaining

Car #3: Lap 3, 1:04 remaining

Car #2: Lap 4, :36 remaining

Car #1: Lap 4, :21 remaining

Street Race 2

Track: Kremlin 1, Moscow
Car: Porsche Cayenne

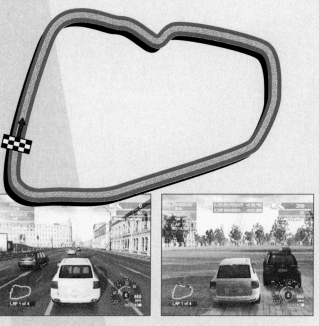

The Kremlin 1 track is no stranger to you after the Overtake track in the Sports Convertible series. Rely on the unbeatable acceleration of your Porsche Cayenne Turbo to overtake the pack and hold a commanding lead.

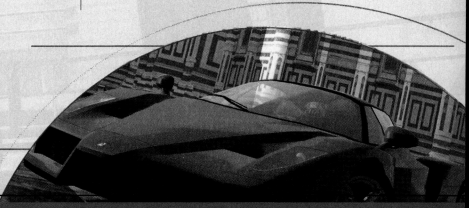

Street Race 3
Track: Red Square 1, Moscow
Car: Porsche Cayenne Turbo

Don't get discouraged if you need a lap or two to catch the leader. Just make sure he's within sight when you start the last lap and you can overtake him with time to spare.

Although eight cars take part in this race, you're really only competing with the other Porsche Cayenne, who starts in the lead. Muscle through for a second-place spot when you come out of the first turn.

It should take only a few turns to catch the leading Porsche. Make the first sharp turn by slowing and following the tire marks in the road precisely.

Use the skid marks in the road to guide you through turns, and take them at lower speeds to guarantee success. There's a pair of acute turns right in the middle of the map where the roads overlap, but you don't need to drop your speed as drastically as you did for the first hairpin turn.

If you get a good line on the third turn, you can probably catch the leader after the fourth (a gradual bend you can accelerate through) and follow close to overtake.

You're almost done now; just one more series of small, controlled turns to take. Watch the aggressive Porsche behind you and keep him from passing through one more lap and you can kiss the SUV series good-bye!

PACIFIC MUSCLE SERIES

The number of trials jumps to 10 for the Pacific Muscle series. You get to drive some of the best retired pocket rockets from the mid-'90s in this category.

Recommended Cars:
Toyota Supra Twin Turbo
Unless you need a car that doesn't slide too much for a tight course, stick with this monster until you have enough Kudos to upgrade. It can get you through most every challenge up through the Silver level.

Nissan Skyline GT-R
Every American racer laments Nissan not exporting this car to the States, so do the next best thing: drive it in this game. This very quick, well-balanced car helps out a lot in the Hard and Expert challenges, so wait until you buy it to tackle them. The Evo VII is an equally competitive choice, and its all-wheel drive helps your acceleration and handling.

Street Race 1
Track: The Convention Centres, Hong Kong
Car: Nissan Skyline GT-R

Unfortunately, the RX-7 in the lead can match your speed, so he keeps the head position unless you get lucky enough to pass him in the first turn. Stay on his tail, but hang back and draft off the Supra for a speed boost.

Stay in hot pursuit around these turns by releasing the gas before entry and gliding through them.
You should catch the RX-7 by the last turn of the first lap, about 25 seconds into the race. Guard the lead by checking your rear and blocking if he gets too close.

Street Race 2
Track: Wan Chai Run, Hong Kong
Car: Nissan Skyline GT-R

It's imperative that you take the next two turns correctly to nab first place. Follow tight on the Lancer in the first bend. Go toward the inside when he drifts outward for the second. Tap the brake a little to stay in control, then let yourself drift out naturally toward him. Time it so you rub his side and edge him out to the left for the lead.

Use your car to block narrow passages and be careful when they open up. The guys on your tail are itching to pass for most of the race.

Street Race 3
Track: Harbour Run, Hong Kong
Car: Nissan Skyline GT-R

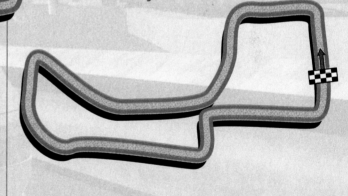

Plan to spend the whole first lap securing your lead. Line up on the left when everyone goes right, and rebound off the Subaru to get right behind the leading Lancer.

It's very, very tough to grab the lead in the first turn of this race... but possible. Line up on the left and aim toward the inside of the turn.

Going into the turn, let off the gas to allow the Supra to pull up next to you. Cut in to the left and accelerate to bounce off the Supra's driver side and into the RX-7. From here, continue into the side of the Subaru that's ahead of the RX-7, which puts you right next to the Lancer at a faster clip than he is able to retain. Pass him at the end of the bridge by nudging him toward the outside. If you're lucky, he'll spin out and lose major time.

It's more likely that you'll have to pull in line after the first turn and endure a few laps before getting a crack at first place. The Lancer and RX-7 or Subaru run ahead and fight for position while you watch from 200 feet back. They're both excellent drivers, so follow their moves to keep up.

Eventually, around the start of the third lap, you catch up right behind the Lancer and have a shot at the lead.

Cone Challenge
Track: Sakuragicho, Yokohama
Car: Mitsubishi Lancer Evolution VII

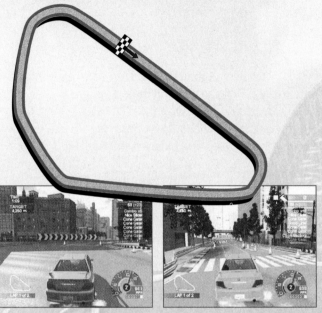

This is a nice, simple Cone Challenge that gives you a chance to try the Lancer Evo VII. It's the perfect car for the track, thanks to its awesome handling and quick acceleration. Throw in a power slide between gates five and six, then again between 11 and 12.

To get the score you need, your combo has to transcend both laps. The last few cone gates at the end of the first lap can be troublesome. Force a brief slide between the four gates leading to the finish line, then gun it to the finish for the Clean Section bonus. Don't slow down much in these slides—keep them short to maintain good velocity.

Hot Lap

Track: Shinko Park, Yokohama
Car: Mitsubishi Lancer Evolution VII

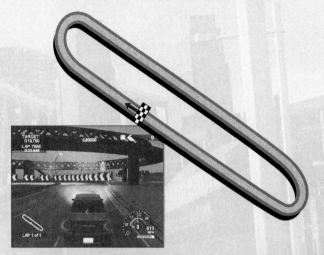

This tiny course has two identical sharp turns. Stay on the right side coming out of the auto start, and start feathering the brake just before you hit the tire marks in the road. Keep a little pressure on the brake and work the gas to keep yourself planted as you take this bend as tightly as possible. Squeaking tires mean lost time, so you don't want to hear them. End up at about 7.1 seconds for your partial-lap marker time.

It's the same deal across the track. Come in at under 13 seconds for this next partial-lap marker to have a shot at the win.

One on One

Track: Seaside Loop, Yokohama
Car: Nissan Skyline GT-R

Once out of the gate, pull up alongside the RX-7. When your nose clears the driver's side of his rear bumper, give him a little love tap with your fender and he'll go careening off to the left. Straighten out and round the corner for a *huge* lead.

The rest of the turns are pretty similar, so take them by slowing just a tad to keep in control and not sliding too much. The RX-7 is in hot pursuit and can overtake you if you dog it too much or run into a few walls in the curves.

Street Race 4

Track: Yokohama Bay Tour, Yokohama
Car: Nissan Skyline GT-R

These next two Street Races are tough because you have to really hang in there for a couple of laps, whether you have the lead or are chasing it. Getting good position from the start is a good first step. Take off and stay left to pass a few guys in the first turn. Don't charge into the corner full-on, but look for a decent hole, and slide into the competition so you don't lose control.

Make a play to advance two or three more cars in the next turn so you end up in second place. Again, stay to the left and work the inside. It may take you several tries (and resets) to make this work just right, but you end up within reach of the lead car and can overtake it in the next couple of turns. If you don't want to end up chasing down super-fast cars for two laps of flawless driving, this is the only other way.

Street Race 5

Track: Minato Mirai, Yokohama
Car: Mitsubishi Lancer Evolution VII

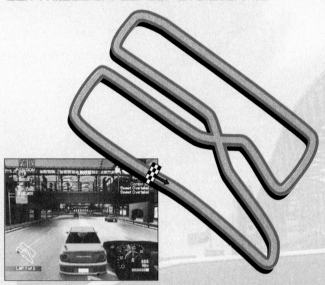

Overtake two cars, or a third if you can do it, by the time you hit the initial turn. Get in line behind the rest of the pack—they all follow almost exactly the same path.

This course has two tight oval turns pretty close together. While it's a good place to lose speed and control, it's also a good spot to overtake other cars that are doing so. Slide in behind the number 3 car in the curve before the first hairpin. Make your move to third coming out of the sharp oval, then draft and overtake the Lancer (or whoever is in that place at the time) to capture second place. Depending on how far the lead car has gotten, you may catch him before the first lap is up.

Speed Camera

Track: Speed Camera Track 1, Hong Kong
Car: Nissan Skyline GT-R

Street Race 6

Track: Admiralty, Hong Kong
Car: Nissan Skyline GT-R

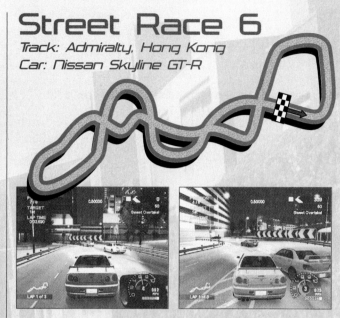

Again, focus on getting the lead—that's your task for most of this final Street Race. Fortunately, the concrete divider in the track creates a real mess early on that you can bust through for good position. Aim for fourth-place going into and second-place coming out of the tunnel.

Pick the manual transmission for the Skyline if you haven't already; it helps you accelerate better and saves time between shifts. Accelerate slowly down the ramp and drop to second gear when the sharp turn starts.

Follow the leader into the concrete bridges. Slow a little, but keep enough speed to pass the head car here. Look for your opening near the end of the bridge. When the path is clear, wedge yourself through, even if it means hitting the wall. Squeeze against your rival to stabilize yourself.

Round the bend tight to the inside near the middle of second gear, then accelerate out, shifting right when the engine is about to redline. Get into fifth gear a couple of seconds before the camera goes off as the car tops out at 119 in fourth.

ROADSTER SERIES

This series has eleven challenges dedicated to these glorified go-karts.

Recommended Car:
AC 427 MKIII
Get a hold of the MKIII to help you through some of these trials. It's great for the Street Races in this series.

Timed Run 1
Track: Opera House View, Sydney
Car: AC 427 MKIII

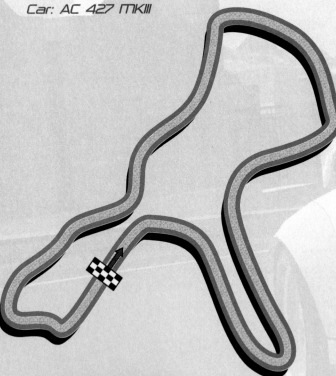

The second turn is a hairpin; take it in the 40-50 mph range with a slide. The MKIII has great power-sliding potential, so use it to make the time on this track.

Three similar turns are next. They're not broad enough to take full-on; regulate your speed heading into them so you don't have to brake hard and drop valuable speed.

Turn one is broad, so you need only mild braking to take it cleanly from full speed.

You should be at about the halfway point on the clock when you come around the last turn. Remember that this track began with a rolling start, so you're expected to make equal time on each lap.

Cone Challenge 1

Track: Under the Bridge, Sydney
Car: AC 427 MKIII

You're faster than anyone here, so take advantage right out of the gate. Gun it up to the first turn and make a go for the lead. Rub up on the two head cars if you need to.

Once you have the lead, the rest of this course is a cinch in the MKIII. You can slow down to take the next two turns at your leisure thanks to your killer acceleration coming out of them.

See the Compact Sports series to revisit the layout on this track; it's the same Cone Challenge, just with two laps. Combo them together with power slides between the longer stretches to make the grade.

Combo in the two uphill jumps for some extra Kudos. Slide a little on the way out of the hill to keep the combo going, but slow down enough that you don't kick your rear into the wall.

Street Race 1

Track: Downtown Short, Sydney
Car: AC 427 MKIII

Timed Run 2

Track: Harbour Bridge, Sydney
Car: AC 427 MKIII

Car #4: Lap 1, 1:59 remaining

Car #3: Lap 2, 1:28 remaining

Car #2: Lap 3, :41 remaining

Car #1: Lap 3, :07 remaining

This one's another auto-start track, and you've seen it before. Check the One on One race in the Coupe series for more track particulars. Aim for the low side of 55 seconds to make this one in Expert mode. Make every turn as tight as the AC allows, and drift a little to take some of the heat off your entry.

Timed Run 3

Track: Princes Street Long, Edinburgh
Car: AC 427 MKIII

The first part of this track is taken from the Princes Street course in the Sport Activity series. The MKIII can take most of these corners with minimal braking. Take a few practice laps so you know where to use a brake drift.

Overtake 1

Track: Hickson Run, Sydney
Car: AC 427 MKIII

If you stick with the MKIII, you can just catch the leader of this race on Expert difficulty.

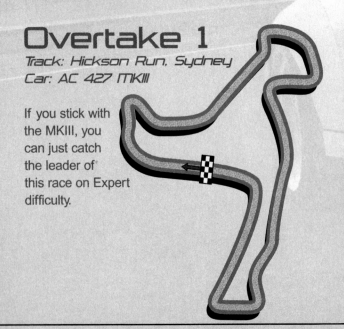

Heading up the small hill exactly halfway around the track, don't slow down—you can make it through here on a clean line. Just stay to the right to make the next bend at the top.

The Grassmarket Eight is another repeater from the Sport Utility series. It's a fun Cone Challenge with the MKIII because it can fishtail like mad and accelerate through just about any pair of cone gates to link a combo.

Slow to about 50 mph into the little hook in the track's southwest corner. From here, roll around to the left and make the last bend just barely touching the outside wall. You want about two minutes on the clock when you exit the turn to make the first lap time a good one.

Cone Challenge 2
Track: Grassmarket Eight, Edinburgh
Car: AC 427 MKIII

If you can't seem to pair up all the gates, toss in a slide for an easy combo. Just give the directional pad a flick in one direction and tap the brake. If you do it right, a couple Kudos pop up in your combo window. It's the next-best way to string tricks and cone gates together for a decent score.

One on One

Track: Grassmarket East, Edinburgh
Car: AC 427 MKIII

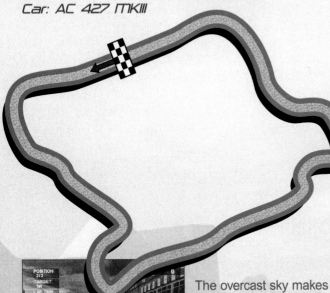

The overcast sky makes this a crazy race for both you and your rival if you don't watch your speed through the corners. You can out-accelerate him from the starting line.

For the rest of the race, you're only one step ahead of your opponent.

Expect him to pass once or twice, but stay close and you can return the favor without much trouble. Watch your map to anticipate turns, as the darkness and rain obscure your long-distance sight.

Street Race 2

Track: Ponte Vecchio, Florence
Car: AC 427 MKIII

This race is really more of a one-on-one between you and the other MKIII. You start on the inside track, so take the lead in the first turn.

You don't have to drive a flawless race to win here, but you do need to keep your twin close. Play leapfrog with him for first place and don't be afraid to ding up his flimsy aluminum body to get position. Wait for him to take turns ahead of you at a slower speed and stay on the gas to T-bone his side door. Do whatever it takes to edge him out; just be sure you have a clean reach at the finish before the final turn.

Speed Camera

Track: Speed Camera Track 1, Florence
Car: AC 427 MKIII

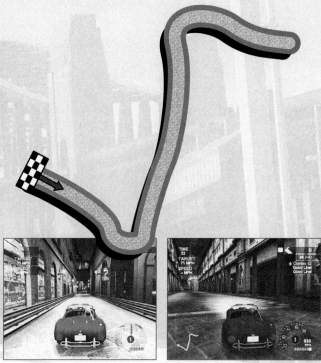

Street Race 3

Track:
Battistero 2,
Florence
Car: AC 427
MKIII

This time your AC-driving rival has a first-place start, so you have to catch him. Accelerate into second place before the turn and start following the leader's racing line precisely.

Don't worry about gaining speed until you start to make the second turn. Take the first at a leisurely 30 or 40 mph and stay on the left.

You should catch up to him about halfway around the track. Look for a good corner, then work up a controlled collision to pass him. The super-tight turn in the track's southern tip is perfect for this.

Brake to around 50 and cut across the inside of the final turn at that speed. (Though this isn't critical because your acceleration is so good.) Now take off hard down the stretch and you'll reach the finish line in time to meet or potentially exceed your goal.

CLASSICS SERIES

This series consists of 11 races starring popular sports cars from the '60s and '70s.

Recommended Cars:
Ferrari 275 GTB
The 275 sports the best combination of speed, handling, and acceleration in the series. Plus, chicks dig Ferraris.

Lancia Stratos
If you're having trouble on tighter tracks, the Lancia's great handling will help you through. Consider it a safety if you get stuck.

Jam on the gas until you approach the small jog. Let off the gas about 100 feet before the turn, then accelerate lightly to keep your back wheels from sliding as you gently work the steering wheel.

Hug the inside railing tightly on this next turn to save precious seconds. Pull a mild slide across the broad curve that follows, just meter the gas to keep your nose pointed parallel to the road. You might finish only tenths of a second ahead of the requirement, but a win is a win. And this one's worth five grand in bonus Kudos.

Hot Lap 1

Track: Las Ramblas, Barcelona
Car: Ferrari 275 GTB

Take off down the straightaway and keep to the track's left side. Take the corner ahead slowly and on the inside rather than sliding through; it's pretty narrow. Don't spend more than nine seconds getting to where this curve straightens out.

Timed Run

Track: Catedral, Barcelona
Car: Ferrari 275 GTB

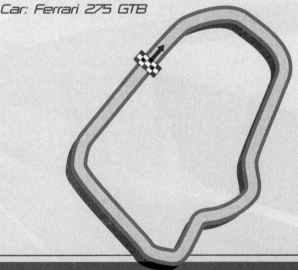

Take this long, first curve without sliding by regulating your speed. Sliding in a long turn such as this one costs you lots of time. Stay close to the right side and keep the tires planted.

The road corners sharply after the next turn; follow the tire treads in the pavement and slow to about 45 mph for a smooth transition. Don't over-steer here or you won't be pointed in the right direction to make this tricky line. Brake lightly going into the turn and, once you round the corner, coast through until you can straighten out to accelerate.

You need about 10 seconds on the clock when exiting the second-to-last turn in the second lap. You can take the last curve without braking if you make a line across the inside of the track and drift outward.

Street Race 1

Track: Place de Jaume, Barcelona
Car: Ferrari 275 GTB

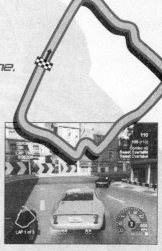

Stick to the tried-and-true method of getting the early lead—it's lot easier to hold than gain later. Cross the initial stretch to the right side, and bounce off the lead cars in the first turn and overtake.

Little slides through this wave-like road pattern ahead build up your Kudos combo and keep you from hitting walls at once. Don't brake, just work the gas on and off to adjust your line.

Take it easy in the next bend; brake lightly and glide through. Don't worry about your lead—it's pretty secure by now.

PRIMA'S OFFICIAL STRATEGY GUIDE

This S-curve is a little trickier as you can lose your balance easily if you take it too hot. After making the first turn on the far right (sticking close to the wall), stay straight and follow the tire treads in the road directly across to the next curve. Brake a little through here and make the right turn smoothly to stay pointed in the right direction when you emerge.

One on One 1

Track: Catalan Challenge, Barcelona
Car: Ferrari 275 GTB

This track is perfect for smooth, controlled drifting in the Ferrari. Overtake the Porsche out of the gate and make the first turn near the track's center-left to get a good, light slide into the next stretch.

Take the light bend on the course's western edge inside with little to no drifting to conserve most of your momentum. Use the straightaway to build up speed past 130 mph before slowing 80 mph for the next curve.

Look out for the offset part of the track in the southeast corner. It doesn't show up as much on the track, but you need to slow significantly to make it through. If your rival is close behind, block up as much of the lane as you can so you don't get passed. Then out-accelerate him.

Set up on the left for the next tight turn, then again for the hairpin loop in the northeast. Meter your speed down to about 75 and hold it throughout this bend to get a good, clean line.

Hot Lap 2
Track: Grassmarket West, Edinburgh
Car: Ferrari 275 GTB

Cone Challenge
Track: Lothian Road Eight Long, Edinburgh
Car: Ferrari 275 GTB

You're back to one lap for this Cone Challenge, whose track is sort of a longer, mutated version of the last Edinburgh Cone Challenge. To do the lap perfectly and get the big score, you won't have to do much more than drive fast and cleanly.

You raced a track just like this in the last series, so it's just a matter of learning your new car's idiosyncrasies to succeed here. Take a few practice runs and see how hard you can push the Ferrari in the various turns. You'll know to take it easy after you get up close and personal with a few walls.

Here are a few places to slide through to keep that combo moving. The rest of the race takes care of you with Good Line and Clean Section bonuses, but go the extra mile in the southeast and northwest corners.

The back half of the track can be taken at higher speeds than the front, so when pacing yourself, don't think of it as half and half. If you're in the neighborhood of 35 seconds at the very bottom of the map, you're looking good.

Overtake

Track: Terrace Sprint, Edinburgh
Car: Ferrari 275 GTB

The dark streets make turns hard to see here, but there aren't that many of them. Go all out and try to overtake all six cars on this course—the competition's pretty light.

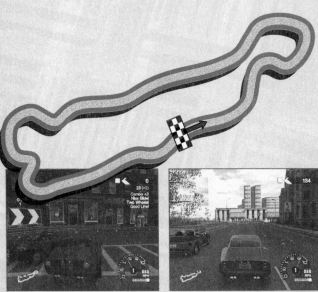

Car #4: Lap 1, 2:16 remaining

Car #3: Lap 1, 2:02 remaining

Car #2: Lap 2, 1:24 remaining

Car #1: Lap 2, 1:11 remaining

One on One 2

Track: Princes Street Long, Edinburgh
Car: Ferrari 275 GTB

If you can throw the opposing Ferrari off in the first stretch here, you'll have a little advantage as you work through this rainy race. Get to the right and beat him to the inside of the first turn. See if you can't nudge him toward the railing in the process.

The competition follows you closely throughout the race, so there's not a lot of room for screw-ups. If you stay in control, don't mess up too many turns, and keep your patience over the three laps, you probably won't even know he's there.

Hot Lap 3

Track: Barri Gotic, Barcelona
Car: Ferrari 275 GTB

Back in Barcelona, this Hot Lap is only one trip around an extended version of the series' first Time Trial. The name of the game for the first two turns is passive drifting. Let the back go out a little to tighten the turns, and brake only if you're skidding out.

PGR 2

This part should look familiar–take the long curve with minimal sliding and shoot for a partial-lap time of about 30 seconds at the marker.

You should hit 100 mph by the time you get to the white lines that separate the turn from the final straightaway. Avoid major turning movements as you accelerate down the strip and you'll hit your goal.

Working through the last tricky spot of the race, head into the small opposing curves on a nearly straight line. Nudge around the corner with a tap on the steering wheel and make the last turn to meet the maximum time.

Street Race 3

Track: Las Ramblas, Barcelona
Car: Ferrari 275 GTB

This is the second time you've raced on this small track; this time it's a five-lapper. You can get second place pretty easily in the first turn, then overtake the GTO on the course shortly thereafter.

Watch for the short jog in the track. Use the first lap to get re-acquainted and don't worry about getting overtaken. You develop a commanding lead in the straightaways that practically can't be beaten.

Speed Camera

Track: Speed Camera Track 1, Barcelona
Car: Ferrari 275 GTB

Accelerate up to 80 mph along the right side of the track and keep building speed through the turn. Pause for a second (about where the checkerboard pattern shows up in the road) to get a tighter turn radius, but get back on the gas and hug the left girder along the curve.

SPORTS COUPE SERIES

This is the biggest series yet. You get to pilot some exotic sports cars in this 13-part showdown.

Recommended Car: Morgan Aero 8, TVR Tamora

The Aero 8 is the most versatile car that still accelerates well enough to dominate the Street Races. But if you have the Kudos Tokens (which you should), the Tamora's acceleration and handling are a real blessing in Overtake and Speed Camera courses. You can get by with either if you're on a budget, though.

The Morgan slides really well, so take advantage in the longer curves. The biggest problem here is reining in the Aero's power at the right times. Learn to let off the gas and feather the brake into turns earlier for better success.

Timed Run

Track: Gamla Stan Loop, Stockholm
Car: Morgan Aero 8

This track is a throwback to the old Compact Sports series, Street Race 2. Refer to that section for a quick look at the track layout. With the rolling start, you need to pull a third of the time per lap (just under 52 seconds each).

Overtake 1

Track: Northern, Stockholm
Car: TVR Tamora

This race is a little easier with the faster, tighter Tamora, so go with it if you bought it. Here's what your schedule should look like to just barely catch the lead car at the end:

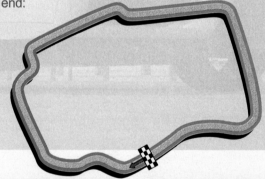

Car #4: Lap 1, 2:04
remaining

Car #3: Lap 1, 1:37
remaining

Car #4: Lap 1, 2:04 remaining

Car #3: Lap 1, 1:37 remaining

Street Race 1

Track: Bridges, Stockholm
Car: TVR Tamora

Even though this track is lousy with short, tight stretches and narrow turns, the high-speed Tamora eats it up. Get to the inside out of the start (if you've learned anything by now, it's always to work inside-out). Brake late into the turn and cut in front of the pack. You don't have to use another car for support unless you fall a little behind, which is okay.

The track's eastern side consists of several narrow sections strung together. Even if you bump and grind along the sharp turns here, you can block any rivals from passing by keeping your bulky body in the way. Keep in control and block with your rear bumper and quarter panels.

Things open up again up once you round the corner. Only one or two cars give realistic pursuit if you've driven well so far. They can't pass you unless you screw up, though.

There's a nasty notch on the track's west side as well. Take it slowly and swing wide to block the lane—it's another narrow one. A few more basic curves follow, but you're about done.

One on One 1

Track: Northern 3, Stockholm
Car: TVR Tamora

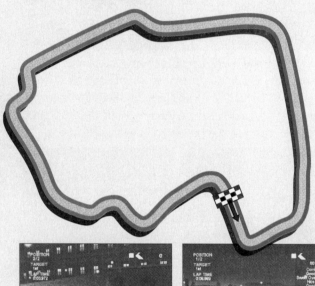

You may be surprised to see this big TVR Tamora match your acceleration, but he can! You have the inside track at the start, however, which means you get to squeak into the lead around the first bend.

With your place established, you're good to go for the rest of the race. Don't give the TVR Tamora any room; he's always lingering behind closer than you think. Don't give even an inch or he'll take it.

Overtake 2

Track: Warehouse Loop, Yokohama
Car: TVR Tamora

You must overtake five cars in the allotted time, so follow this pacing:

Car #5: Lap 1, 2:24 remaining

Car #4: Lap 1, 2:00 remaining

Car #3: Lap 2, 1:15 remaining

Car #2: Lap 2, :21 remaining

Car #1: Lap 3, :04 remaining

Street Race 2

Track: Kishamichi, Yokohama
Car: TVR Tamora

Hitting one or both from behind, drive them into the opposite girder to slow them down, and accelerate away. One may break free early and get ahead of you, so stay right on his tail.

Overtake the temporary leader within one or two turns, then just worry about making it through the course in the rain. Brake for your turns a little earlier and check your mirror frequently. The pursuing cars are both very fast (one of them is a copy of yours, after all).

Break to the left out of the start and pass up the pack that's lagging back here. Gently cut over to the right while you pick up steam. Don't slow down until you face the turn's inside corner. There should be two cars right in front of you braking into the turn.

Cone Challenge

Track: Downtown, Yokohama
Car: Morgan Aero 8

You have two laps to get the relatively low minimum score on this Cone Challenge, so it's not too tough. Use the more drift-friendly Aero 8 here if you have it.

Also, you need lots of speed to link the gates on the bridge, so give yourself time to build it beforehand.

Speed Camera

Track: Speed Camera Track 1, Yokohama
Car: TVR Tamora

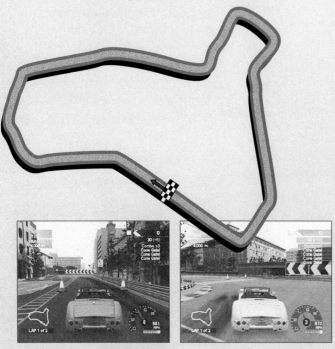

A couple of spots are tricky to nail when combo-ing. The first is in the southeast corner. Come through the previous gate as you slow down and edge the wheel gently left to slide through the perpendicular one on the opposite side of the turn. This way you have enough speed to make the next gate on the left.

Pick this one up without even trying. Accelerate leisurely to the sharp bend and take the corner at around 40 for a safe bet. Now run it up through the stretch, jogging slightly over for the offset, and clear with speed to spare.

One on One 2

Track: Warehouse Loop, Yokohama
Car: TVR Tamora

If you do get passed, overtake your rival by drafting him. Then give him a taste of sidewall to mess him up so you can recapture the lead.

Timed Run

Track: Hennessey Run, Hong Kong
Car: TVR Tamora

Get to the right side of the track out of the starting gate. Your opponent has the inside this time, so be careful he doesn't ram you as you take the turn. Cut in front of him and force him to slow down to take the lead.

Take advantage of the Tamora's handling to cut off these turns across the shoulder. Your opponent has excellent acceleration and will pass you in the turns if you don't keep up your speed.

Despite this track's cramped feel, take it at high speeds with controlled slides and braking. Get through the first turn by braking lightly when you're over the tire marks and cutting inward. You should be at about 17 seconds when you come out of the second curve.

Take the next two curves in one continuous motion. Get off the gas in the first curve and passively drift a little as you work the accelerator to keep the wheels planted. Get a nice line that won't hurt your speed. You should have roughly 24 seconds on the clock after the turn.

The big curve by the Siemens sign is tough to read—it actually closes up on the left once you get around it, so tighten up to veer right on the way out.

The final turn can mess you up pretty badly. When heading up the concrete-walled part of the track, stay to the right and brake a little as you move left to adjust for the wall's position up the hill. You'll get stuck perpendicular to the wall if you hit here, which kills your hopes of a win. If you make it to the corner at about 1:22, you can save exactly half the time for your second lap.

Street Race 3

Track: Admiralty, Yokohama
Car: TVR Tamora

Use your acceleration advantage to take the lead in the first few turns. Once you shed the previous leaders from your tail, they stay pretty far behind.

When you get to the road split, take the underpass on the right. This gives you more space to make a wide turn when you emerge, which conserves your speed.

Be mindful of your speed when navigating the narrow concrete bridges. Hit a wall and you'll get tangled up. It's tough for opponents to pass you here, so a little drop in speed for safety's sake can't hurt.

As always, take downhill curves at especially reduced speed. You don't want to launch off the hill into a wall.

Street Race 5

Track: Cotton Tree Drive, Yokohama
Car: TVR Tamora

Street Race 4

Track: Wan Chai Run, Yokohama
Car: TVR Tamora

Hold off on your bid for the lead until the track widens. The starting bridges are narrow, but slip by on the right to improve your position by a few notches. Now make passes one at a time, drafting behind your prey if need be.

This run is very tame if you are patient about taking the lead. Work the inside through the first turn to get behind the leader. Follow him through turn number two (draft behind him for a speed boost) and make your move on the inside of turn three. With the lead in hand, only five laps with a few mild curves stand between you and the win.

When in third, follow the lead cars as they lead you on what could be a whole lap or two. You have several potential opportunities to pass in the turns, but wait for the one you know will work. A failed attempt can leave you way behind when the dust settles. Tackle the leaders one at a time and you're good to go.

AMERICAN MUSCLE SERIES

Welcome to the world of V8 engines and cars that handle like tuna boats—it may take you some time to adjust after driving the little Pacific Muscle cars. This set of 14 tracks starts off in the good old Midwest.

Recommended Car: Corvette Sting Ray

Because the Corvette drives like it's on ice full time, drive it gingerly to get results. Pretend it's a real Corvette and you don't want to get it scratched or over-driven, and you'll do well. Mild changes to your speed with light gas and brakes are a must. Also pick up the SVT Cobra or the Chevrolet Camaro SS if you can afford it. They help on tighter tracks where decent handling is a must.

Street Race 1

Track: Miracle Mile, Chicago
Car: Corvette Sting Ray

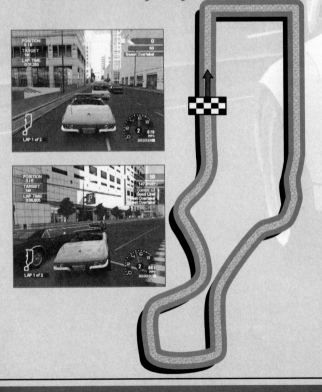

Take the lead early and you'll have a much easier time in Chicago. Cut to the right and go around the pack so you're just behind the second-place car in the turn. Lean on him just a little to make the turn tighter, but don't lose control. Pull up behind the lead car in the straightaway.

Stay close and be patient as you follow through the next few turns. Take the loose S-curve by dropping off the gas early and gliding tight across both inside girders. Now it's time to pass the leader.

Fade to the right as you head under the tracks. Get close enough to cut the leader off in the turn for this to work. Take it sharp and at full speed on the far inside, then pull to the right to rub up against the lead car and push him aside.

Stay cautious through the last few turns and you'll be on the way to a comfortable lead. Slow down extra early to make the sharp turn at the bridge. It comes up fast, so plan ahead. The pack of cars following you earlier is now slowing up the former first-place runner. Good news for you.

Street Race 2

Track: Chicago River Tour, Chicago
Car: Corvette Sting Ray

The trick to driving the 'Vette lies in gradual movements. Throughout the track, engage your steering, braking, and acceleration very gradually unless you're trying for a big power slide. But don't get passed by being too granny-minded. Check the rearview constantly to stay awake.

Cone Challenge 1

Track: North Wabash Overpass, Chicago
Car: Chevrolet Camaro SS

Same drill on this track. Get to the inside in the first turn and overtake the leader right away.

You need a staggering 15,000 Kudos on this track, which means two flawless trips around through the cone gates. And the Camaro is about the best thing going on a setup like this. It's not blindingly fast, but you don't need speed here. You need to whip up a slide and keep good lines to maintain your combos.

When dealing with the cone gates and bridges along the track's southwest end, to make it through the two cone gates that are spaced completely apart on the track, slide through both. Come in on a hard angle on the right one, cut the wheel left to slide through it until you're facing across to the left one. The slide gives you more time to maintain the combo and gives you better position entering the gates.

Make for the left-hand bridge when you emerge from the second gate. It gets you closer to the next cone gate on the opposite side.

Hot Lap 1

Track: Wells & Lake, Chicago
Car: Corvette Sting Ray

You don't have to use the Sting Ray here if you're not comfortable with its skatey driving, but its acceleration keeps you from losing time in the turns. Try the SVT or SS if you're not getting it.

As with most Hot Laps, this one's reserved for those who can play a course dozens of times to make every turn just right. The ideal is to not brake at all–take every turn by simply slowing and hitting the line right. Because you're driving the speedy 'Vette, pull a *Blues Brothers* below the train tracks and clear 100 mph to give yourself some breathing room.

One on One
Track: In the Loop, Chicago
Car: Corvette Sting Ray

It's two 'Vettes in the rain on this track, which means especially cautious driving all around. Grab the lead in the usual manner—take the inside and drift out into your rival to stay in line.

The hairpin turn on the far-east side is actually great to take on a slide with the rain falling. Slow to about 70 mph before you cut in hard to the left and you can swing perfectly through the turn and come out facing straight on the other side.

Street Race 3
Track: Wells & Lake, Chicago
Car: Corvette Sting Ray

How's your memory? Back at the Wells & Lake track, this Street Race would be a piece of cake in the daylight. But it's in the dead of night, so use the map and your memory to anticipate the tight turns your lights can't illuminate.

Take the lead in the second turn by getting into second place in the first. Follow the other 'Vette and slip past by exceeding his speed on the inside of the bend. You should know the track by heart if you pulled off the Expert Hot Lap before!

Take all three turns in the northwestern square with that trademark Corvette slide for a bigger combo and a better chance of keeping your chain going. Use it to nail the hairpin and get through the tight cone gates on the east end.

Cone Challenge 2

Track: Northside Slide, Washington D.C.
Car: Corvette Sting Ray

Street Race 4

Track: Capitol Thrill, Washington D.C.
Car: Corvette Sting Ray

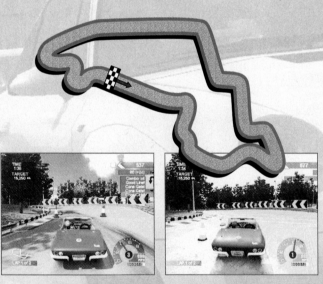

They don't call it the Northside Slide for nothing. The Corvette gives you the acceleration to bridge several of the lengthy cone gate gaps, and the slippery-bottomed car makes some key connections through drifting.

One of the dangers associated with driving the Corvette in traffic is that the slightest tap from an opponent can send you into an uncontrolled slide. That's why it's best to get out ahead from the start and have a clean track ahead, so do it again here in the first turn.

Set up on the left side from the start and move gradually right. Before getting to the turn, line to the left of the inside girder and aim to meet the lead cars as they come around the bend. Veer off the second-place vehicle and across the lead car to move into first place. You may have to do a little damage-control recovery, but pull out and you're in good shape to finish out the lap.

Hot Lap 2
Track: Square Dancin', Washington D.C.
Car: Corvette Sting Ray

Although the turns are reversed on the way back up, this track is more or less symmetrical, so you want to be right around :39 when you hit the halfway point at the bottom. Also, accelerate slowly when you hit the straightaways so you don't end up spinning your wheels in the rain-soaked street.

Timed Run
Track: Up and Over, Washington D.C.
Car: Corvette Sting Ray

Slow into the first hairpin turn and take it tight around the inside. Don't bother trying to slide through; it's a very acute angle. Accelerate slowly into the stretch and look to be at around :17 coming out of the second bend.

Get a wide reach on all these turns to minimize skidding in the rain. You can slide a little and still get a really good line, so leave yourself room to drift out on the opposite sides of these curves.

Street Race 6

Track: North Wabash Overpass, Chicago
Car: Corvette Sting Ray

If you're at about :42 out of the northernmost point on the track, you are right on target to leave half your time for lap 2. Swing around tight on this turn and gun it when you round the next corner. Don't slow for the final turn until you get to the break in the tire streaks on the pavement.

Street Race 5

Track: Capitol Thrill 2, Washington D.C.
Car: Corvette Sting Ray

The pack closes off any attempt to take a lead in this first bend, so slip into third place on the right wall and stay on the leaders. Hard acceleration in the next stretch gives you the opening inside the next turn.

Jump on the gas and squeeze between the cars that flank you. Move right and follow the car line to the turn at full speed. Bump the line of cars by ramming the back-right flank of the car ahead. This creates a billiard-ball-collision effect on the vehicles that messes a few of them up. Get as far ahead as you can and follow the leaders.

The next series of turns each give you a new chance to go inside for a position jump, so leapfrog cars from curve to curve until you eventually take the leader. You probably will overtake just before completing the first lap of four. Now your toughest obstacle is the extreme dark that obscures turns. Use your map more than your road view and look for yellow arrows that signal upcoming curves and their directions.

As your competition comes up on you, go ahead and play some defense to fend 'em off. If you see a hood pop up behind you, line up in front to make him give you a speed-boosting bump. Or cut across the track to flick him into the side rail.

Speed Camera

Track: Speed Camera Track 1,
Chicago
Car: Corvette Sting Ray

It doesn't matter how you drive this beginning part (up to the southwest corner), but get on the far right before heading across the bridge. Turn at around 65 mph and accelerate, making a tight cut over the left side of the bridge. This should keep you from sliding significantly.

Stay to the left side of this curve so you can bear right for the final leg. Just tap the control pad to make the light turn so you don't skid out.

Street Race 7

Track: Lower Wacker Run,
Chicago
Car: Corvette Sting Ray

Think ahead to get good position in the first lap. Take the first mild right passing one or two of the last few cars. As cars start lining up for the next right turn, go outside instead of inside to pass the fifth- and fourth-place cars. This way, you're set up to pass cars 2 and 3 on the inside of the upcoming left turn. This puts you on the leader's tail. Once you're within about 50 feet, catch him in one of the upcoming corners.

The darkness is the worst on this track. Look out for the huge, concrete structures and pillar dividers in the road; they creep up when you're in the lead and there's not much light on the track. Try turning up the brightness on your TV if stuff is jumping out of the shadows.

PRIMA'S OFFICIAL STRATEGY GUIDE

SUPER CARS SERIES

Made up of the kinds of cars you see in rap videos and Beverly Hills, the Super Cars series features 14 tough trials.

> ## Recommended Cars:
> ### TVR Tuscan Speed 6
> Great acceleration and handling.
>
> ### Dodge Viper GTS
> The car to use when you need lots of headroom on the speedometer.

The long, wide turn shouldn't require any braking or slowing if you take it just right, but let off the gas just a tad if you're really flying and nearing the back girder.

Don't slide thorough this one, even though it's pretty wide—you'll lose valuable time. Take it under light braking and check your lap time at the starting gate.

Timed Run

Piazza della Repubblica, Florence
Car: TVR Tuscan Speed 6
Going six times around this course at an average of 23.3 seconds each is certainly not easy. Some practice helps you get in the groove to nail this one.

Overtake 1

Track: Piazza della Signoria 2, Florence
Car: Dodge Viper GTS
The Viper's speed will help you win this tight race. Here's what it should look like:

Take the first two mild turns at full speed. Cut the corner as close as you can without crashing.

Car #7: Lap 1, 2:43 remaining

Car #6: Lap 1, 2:24 remaining

Car #5: Lap 2, 1:58 remaining

Follow the tire treads and brake lightly to get the right line in the next turn. Your clock should be at about six seconds after the turn.

Car #4: Lap 2, 1:45 remaining

Car #3: Lap 2, 1:11 remaining

Car #2: Lap 3, :53 remaining

Car #1: Lap 4, :04 remaining

One on One 1

Track: Piazza della Signoria 1, Florence
Car: Dodge Viper GTS

Draft behind your opponent's Viper through the first two turns and pace him as you approach the bridge. Unless he screws up, you probably won't be able to pass him yet.

Make your move toward the inside and block up the southwest corner of the track as you make your turn in the southwest corner. If he comes back, use the cramped corners and narrow stretches of this Florence track to scrape him off your tail.

Speed Camera

Track: Speed Camera Track 1, Florence
Car: TVR Tuscan Speed 6

Accelerate to about 65-70 mph out of the gate and hold as you drive through the opening of the curve. Stay near the left-center, and just before you see the rest of the track appear from between the buildings, start accelerating hard from about 70 mph. You will just clear the next corner by hopping the rumble strip and make it to the finish to just meet you goal.

Street Race 1

Track: Ponte Vecchio, Florence
Car: TVR Tuscan Speed 6

Take the inside immediately and pass all but the lead two cars in the first turn. The competition leaves a little alley for you to get by on. Cut the number 2 car off into the second turn to take his position.

Stay on the leader's rear end and you'll have an easy shot at overtaking in the next few curves. You may have to wrestle with him a little, but make your move when he slows down to turn and you'll have first place soon enough.

Hot Lap 1

Track: Grassmarket East, Edinburgh
Car: Dodge Viper GTS

You'll need to watch your speed in the first turn so you don't hit the small bump here and fly in to the wall. Regulate up to and through the first two turns then pick up the pace until you reach the hairpin in the southwest corner. The most important lesson here is not to slow down during the upcoming straightaway if you can avoid it. The whole southern edge can be taken with minimal braking—just keep in control and try to push the Viper as hard as it will go in this area.

Hot Lap 2

Track: Terrace Sprint, Edinburgh
Car: Dodge Viper GTS

The Viper's a little skatey, but its speed will help you make the single lap here. Don't let off the gas until the curve in the southwest corner starts to come up.

Because you're often shooting from turn to turn, get into a good rhythm and follow a pattern. Cut a turn on the inside and drift outside, then adjust for the next turn. Most of these are S-shaped patterns, so think about which side you need to set on for the following turn before you've completed the first one.

Street Race 2

Track: Princes Street East, Edinburgh
Car: Dodge Viper GTS

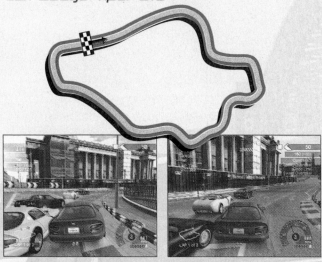

Stay on the gas as you follow the competition into the first turn. Get to the right and look for an opening when the other cars round the bend. There should be room for you to sneak in on the inside and deflect off the second- and third-place cars to get behind the first-place Viper.

If you've done it correctly, you'll be right on his tail. When he widens to make the next turn, scoot by on the inside or force him into a wreck on the outside. Either way, you'll be poised to overtake and establish a good lead before you're halfway through the first lap.

One on One 2

Track: Princes Street Loop, Edinburgh
Car: Dodge Viper GTS

You can use the Viper or the Tuscan here and have a good shot at the win."

Remember to swing the front end out a little before taking sharp turns for a better exit. And keep your speed up by taking the two mild curves at the end of the lap in a virtually straight line. You may hop two wheels up off the shoulder, so don't lose control by making drastic steering movements.

Cumberland Street is just two straightaways connected by a hairpin and one milder turn. Accelerate all the way through the stretches, but start braking early for turns or you'll get buried in the wall.

The night sky makes it tough to read the contour of the hairpin turn on the north end. Use the arrows along the back wall as a guide—make a straight line for the right edge of the arrow sign when you emerge from the first part of the curve. Nudge right once the rest of the turn appears in your headlights.

Hot Lap 3

Track: Cumberland Street, Sydney
Car: Dodge Viper GTS

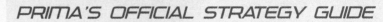
Overtake 2

Track: Downtown Short, Sydney
Car: TVR Tuscan Speed 6

Here's what this quick race looks like if you use the Tuscan:

Car #5: Lap 2,
:51 remaining

Car #4: Lap 2,
:44 remaining

Car #3: Lap 2, :28
remaining

Car #2: Lap 3, :18
remaining

Car #1: Lap 3,
:02 remaining

Car #7: Lap 1,
1:19 remaining

Car #6: Lap 1,
1:07 remaining

Street Race 3

Track: George St. Challenge, Sydney
Car: Dodge Viper GTS

Get on the inside (left) part of the track and overtake the rear few cars through the first turn by passing on the left. Try to drift out into cars ahead and let them absorb the shock as you slide by.

You should end up in second or third place when you hit the straight-away. You won't be able to overtake the Viper in the lead just yet, but stay with him and mimic his moves through the sharp turn at the end of the stretch. You can draft behind him if you get close enough then move in for the overtake.

Stay on the leading Viper and look to overtake in the second half of the first lap. Let him too far ahead and you'll have a hard time catching him later, so get the overtake done early on.

Street Race 5

Track: The Rocks Route, Sydney
Car: Dodge Viper GTS

The trick to staying competitive from the start is, once again, playing off the initial curve. When the competition slows to take the sharp turn, you need to line up a glancing blow off the second-place car (the Viper is already ahead) that will knock you through the turn without you slowing down. Set it up right and you will deflect right off his body panel and into a path behind the first-place Viper. Follow his movements until he makes a mistake or slows enough that you can pass.

Street Race 4

Track: Sydney Harbour, Sydney
Car: Dodge Viper GTS

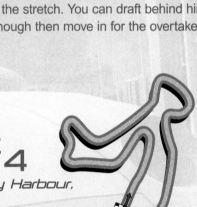

The immediate hairpin turn on this track has the whole race pack slowing down early on, so use the opportunity to ascend the ranks. Glance off the side of a slowing car to propel yourself into second place.

GRAND TOURING SERIES

The exotics here are more show than go (at least compared to the Super Car series), but a couple of gems help you through these 16 challenges.

Recommended Car: Ferrari 575M Maranello

The Maranello doesn't handle as well as the Mercedes in this series, but its acceleration edge is more valuable for some races. Its only weak point is the Cone Challenge, so get the Bentley for that trial if you're bent on finishing it.

Timed Run

Track: Yokohama Honcho dor
Car: Ferrari 575M Maranello

You have to take all eight turns of this simple race perfectly to make the tough time requirement, but they're all the same. Once you figure out the best line for one, it's just a matter of reproducing it. With the Ferrari, slow with light brake pressure and release as you start your turn. Tap the brake again once or twice if you're headed for the wall, but not too much or it'll cost you the race.

The halfway point is a pretty exact indicator of progress here because the track is so balanced, so check yourself and restart if you're off pace.

Overtake 1

Track: Kishamichi, Yokohama
Car: Ferrari 575M Maranello

Drafting behind cars you're about to overtake helps you keep your speed up in this race. Also, try to ride an opponent's side panel through a turn to both overtake him and save seconds on the clock.

Car #7: Lap 1, 3:14 remaining

Car #6: Lap 1, 2:50 remaining

Car #5: Lap 2, 1:57 remaining

Car #4: Lap 2, 1:17 remaining

Car #3: Lap 3, :50 remaining

Car #2: Lap 3, :33 remaining

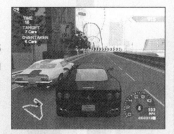

Car #1: Lap 3, :16 remaining

Your contact maneuver may enable one or two trailing cars to slip by while you regain speed, but with your acceleration you can overtake them within seconds. The next two laps are a breeze in first place.

Street Race 1

Track: Yokohama Challenge
Car: Ferrari 575M Maranello

The real kicker on this challenge is overtaking the Mercedes that starts in the lead and can handle like a dream. Thanks to your, shall we say, "moral flexibility," you can crush the heck out of him in the first turn and forget he even exists for the rest of the race.

One on One 1

Track: The Convention Centres, Hong Kong
Car: Ferrari 575M Maranello

Move to the right of the Testarossa and draft briefly behind the Lotus to get additional speed. When you're about to overtake it, move left again and accelerate hard down the track.

Back to a familiar track, and it's an easy one. Just take your opponent on the inside of the first or second turn to get the lead.

The rain makes everything sluggish, including cornering and acceleration. Hit the gas too hard from a slow speed and you spin the tires without making much progress. Expect all your actions to require a little more time.

Mash the gas and line up just a few feet from the left-side girder. The Mercedes swings wide to take the turn and starts to cut in front of your nose. Keep the accelerator smashed down until just before you hit his side, then brake and cut to the left to strike a glancing blow. You skate off in the direction of the track while he's calling AAA on the sidelines.

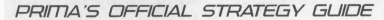

Cone Challenge

Track: Hennessey Road, Hong Kong
Car: Ferrari 575M Maranello

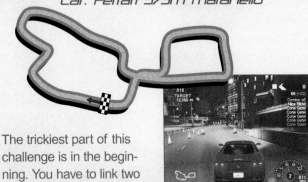

The trickiest part of this challenge is in the beginning. You have to link two cone gates that are just out of your speed range for a cone gate combo. One simple solution is to throw a quick brake drift in to keep the combo going. When you've cleared the fifth gate, hit your brakes for a second and kick the rear out without losing control or changing your line drastically. You should get a small slide bonus that will carry your combo into the sixth gate.

As you work through the middle of the track, use the Maranello's speed and tight handling to dart through the line of gates. Be careful not to make too many harsh steering adjustments or your back end will weave out of control.

That pesky Mercedes is back again, but this time you need to be a little more patient to overtake him. Line up on the left side to start and gun it hard. By the time you reach the corner, the Testarossa should be there to give you a nice cushion off which to glance. Recover smoothly and you end up about five car lengths behind the Mercedes leader.

Follow him as fast as you can. Back off the gas for just a second to make the turn coming out from under the bridge and to take the mild S-curve in the track ahead. In the track's northwest corner, he slows down and swings wide to take the turn. Keep up your speed and cut him off on the inside. Knock him out of the picture with as much of a glancing blow as you can muster at this speed. Recover, accelerate out, and get back up to a decent speed so someone else doesn't pass you!

Street Race 2

Track: Harbour Run, Hong Kong
Car: Ferrari 575M Maranello

Overtake 2

Track: KGB Corner, Moscow
Car: Ferrari 575M Maranello

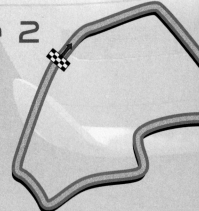

The course here is wide throughout. Rivals try to use the space to get in your way or simply take very good lines in the turns to keep as far ahead as possible.

Take very long, wide approaches to get a good line that involves little to no braking. Cut in slowly and early—you have the space on most of these curves. Aim for the point where the inside girder juts out into the

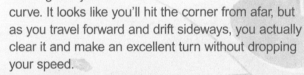

curve. It looks like you'll hit the corner from afar, but as you travel forward and drift sideways, you actually clear it and make an excellent turn without dropping your speed.

Use this wide-approach technique on every turn to make the time requirement.

Hot Lap 1

Track: Red Square 1, Moscow
Car: Ferrari 575M Maranello

This is an extremely tough track because of its length and number of turns. Every corner you don't take just right affects your time in the end, so practice a number of times.

Try setting goals once you get an idea of the layout. Use landmarks such as buildings and the big wall in the park, and set realistic time goals for reaching them. After several runs, you'll know which turns you're taking well and which need work. Set new goals that shave seconds off your time after you've addressed these issues. Also, check to see where you end up on the course at the target time for each run so you can see the end results of your cornering improvement.

 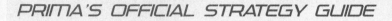

Street Race 3

Track: Kremlin 2, Moscow
Car: Ferrari 575M Maranello

Getting the lead here is pretty easy. Sift through the trailing cars and move behind the leader in the first turn.

Follow the leader into the next turn; when he goes left, go right to get inside. Brake hard and slow down a good deal to get through it—you can pull it off before anyone overtakes you.

A first-place position helps you navigate the tangle of turns ahead. Keep your speed between 50 and 70 mph and take all these without much braking or sliding. The track opens back up again in the northern tip, so you can run a lot faster for the rest of the race.

One on One 2

Track: Speed Freak, Stockholm
Car: Ferrari 575M Maranello

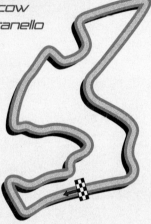

It's time for a little sibling rivalry. Your Ferrari opposition can match your acceleration, so follow him and draft to pick up some more speed. Move inside on the first turn to overtake. Sweep back and forth through the next couple of turns that follow—your rival is probably right on your tail through it all.

Because this race is only one lap, it's best to take it easy enough to just keep your opponent behind you. Make sure you can guarantee yourself a good turn every time even if it's not at the best speed. Check your rear often and block as necessary to get you to the finish line first.

Overtake 3

Track: Place de Jaume, Barcelona

Car: Ferrari 575M Maranello

Take a few laps to learn the course and this one's not too tough.

The easiest way to lose time on this track is excess sliding. Get to a speed where you can make tight turns around the rails. It may not seem like it at the time, but the savings on the clock add up in the end.

Car #7: Lap 1, 1:53 remaining

Car #6: Lap 1, 1:26 remaining

Car #5: Lap 2, 1:19 remaining

The little notch in the southeast corner is a killer. If you take it too fast, you'll spend valuable time wrestling your way out of it. Head into it slowly, cut over sharply, and don't let your back end slide out as you round the inside wall. If you do, you'll be facing back toward the way you came in.

Car #4: Lap 2, 1:00 remaining

Car #3: Lap 3, :41 remaining

Car #2: Lap 3, :37 remaining

Car #1: Lap 3, :27 remaining

One on One 3

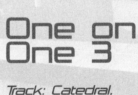

Track: Catedral, Barcelona

Car: Ferrari 575M Maranello

Hot Lap 2

Track: Catalan Challenge, Barcelona

Car: Ferrari 575M Maranello

The lap here is super-short, but you need to complete five of them to win. Because the track is so narrow, the lead is easily defended once gotten.

Follow through the first turn—it's a long bend. In the second turn, get up behind the Ferrari when he slows down and drive him forward toward the opposite wall to throw off his balance. Veer off to the right and keep going as the lead car.

Speed Camera

Track: Speed Camera Track 1, Washington D.C.
Car: Ferrari 575M Maranello

Start on the left and get going to about 60 mph. Turn in toward the first turn, then cut left to take the second corner on the inside.

Just when you round the bend, start accelerating from about 62 mph and clear the last corner close to the girder so you have room to drift outward on the other side. You should be at 92 mph when you hit the point to make 134 at the camera.

Street Race 4

Track: Capitol Thrill 2, Washington D.C.
Car: Ferrari 575M Maranello

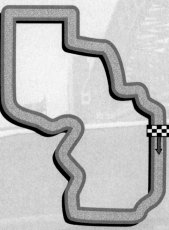

Here's a snazzy trick to hook an early lead in what seems like a jammed course. As you accelerate from the start, get to the center of the track and pass the last few cars. Keep an eye on the Lotus in front of you as you head into the turn.

The Lotus veers to one side partway through the turn, leaving you room to zoom past and cut through the leading three vehicles. You may have to bump the third-place guy on the back to break through the right side.

Head straight out from the line and drift a little to your right to go around the Bentley. Now slide back in front of it to get between the Testarossa and the guardrail for the turn. Glance off the Lotus and get to the right side.

As with most tracks in this series, it's easier to hold the lead than to acquire it. If you make all the turns ahead following the tire marks in the pavement, you won't be passed.

You end up next to the two convertibles, about to overtake them both. The lead car is setting up wide for the turn, so stay on the right (inside) and accelerate hard to meet him. Brake to kick your back out as you nudge his back just enough to throw off his line. He heads off to the left and you're pointed toward the turn exit. You are almost stopped at this point, so cover as much of the track as you can as you accelerate back to speed and take first place.

Street Race 5

Track: The Tour, Washington D.C.
Car: Ferrari 575M Maranello

TRACK SPECIALS SERIES

You've got even more exotic muscle cars to play with during this 17-event series.

> **Recommended Car:**
> **Porsche 911 GT3**
> **and Noble M12 GTO3**
> Use the Porsche for Hot Lap races when you need a good top speed. The Noble is tough to beat for acceleration and can be a big help in Street Races and One on One trials.

Hot Lap 1

Track: Nordschleife 2, Nürburgring
Car: Porsche 911 GT3

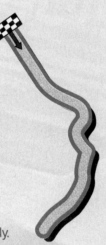

The Porsche has the highest top speed, which helps on the huge initial straightaway. Take the turns at the following approximate speeds for greatest success. Remember that the faster you go, the earlier you have to start slowing down. When decelerating from speeds over 150 mph, don't just let off the gas entirely or you might skid out. Ease it down to about 120 before you drop it completely.

| Turn 1: | Turn 2: | Turn 3: |
| 85-95 mph | 70-80 mph | 70-80 mph |

| Turn 4: | Turn 5: | Turn 6: |
| 85-95 mph | 75-85 mph | 75-85 mph |

Street Race 1

Track: Nordschleife 3, Nürburgring
Car: Noble M12 GTO3

You notice another Noble ahead of you gunning for the lead, so get behind him on the way to the front of the pack. With or even without drafting, you can overtake him before you get to the first turn.

If you're not confident about holding the lead through the bend, stay right behind the other Noble going into the turn and squeak by on the track when he slows down (or pull a small lawn job) to overtake him

Hot Lap 2

Track: Nordschleife 4, Nürburgring Car: Porsche 911 GT3

Stay at top speed all the way down the line until you see the pair of blue signs. Drop just a tiny bit of speed to take the light curve ahead, but keep close to 160 until you can see the main turn in the distance.

Now ease off the gas to enter the turn at around 100–10 mph. Meter your gas through the turn until it's safe to accelerate back to cruising speed.

Be careful coming up the hill that lies ahead. Some idiot put a left turn atop it.

PGR 2

Hot Lap 3

Track: Nordschleife 5, Nürburgring
Car: Porsche 911 GT3

Use the Porsche on this track; you'll need its high top speed to help you through. Once you learn the location of the tricky spots, you should be good to go.

Accelerate hard until you start to go uphill. There's a left turn right at the top, so let off the gas halfway up the hill to make it safely. Don't build too much speed yet; you still have a little tangle of turns to negotiate.

The northern point of the track has a couple more turns you have to take at significantly regulated speed. Stay near the inside of the curves so you can set up for an immediate turn the other way.

One on One 1

Track: Nordschleife 6, Nürburgring
Car: Noble M12 GTO3

The Noble can overtake the Ferrari you're racing with ease, so pass on the left and try to put some space behind you while you can. Your opponent has good speed, so don't dog it too much.

You can ride the striped shoulders without losing too much speed or control. If it helps you get a better line on the turn, use it.

If your rival is trying to pass, put some pressure on his side by leaning into him if you can't block him entirely with your tail. It's difficult for him to break free and pass when you've got him locked down like this.

Street Race 2

Track: Gamla Island Hopping, Stockholm
Car: Noble M12 GTO3

Pass the back few cars and get behind the Porsche leading up to the first turn. Draft for a second and scoot out to the left to take the broad curve.

You can't catch the other M12 ahead yet, so just keep on him as tight as you can. Follow his path through the corkscrew turn and down the next couple of stretches.

If you drive well enough or the leader makes even a small mistake (which he does sometimes in a car that fast), you can overtake before the first lap is out.

Overtake 1

Track: Gamla Oval, Stockholm
Car: Noble M12 GT03

You're not in Nürburgring anymore. The streets of Stockholm are tighter, so brake frequently to make these narrow turns. Pass the seven cars at this rate:

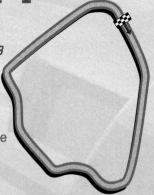

Car #7: Lap 1, 2:02 remaining

Car #6: Lap 1, 1:54 remaining

Car #5: Lap 1, 1:39 remaining

Car #4: Lap 2, 1:20 remaining

Car #3: Lap 3, :41 remaining

Car #2: Lap 3, :35 remaining

Car #1: Lap 3, :14 remaining

Timed Run 1

Track: Bridges, Stockholm
Car: Noble M12 GT03

Be careful but aggressive with Stockholm's cramped curves; two laps make for a lot of opportunities to nail a wall. Cheat toward the inside more than the outer edge when setting up for turns and rely on the Noble's stickiness to keep you in line.

On the map's northernmost side, what looks like two separate turns is just a small offset in the road linked by mild curves. Shoot through these on practically a straight line. This is a good place to lose lots of time if you take it wrong.

90

Now play defense. Check your rearview every few seconds to check for a pass attempt.

Hot Lap 4
Track: Island Hop, Stockholm
Car: Noble M12 GTO3

This track is very similar to the Bridges track you just raced. The rain makes it hard to judge speed through turns, but you have to keep your velocity up while still adhering to the race line if you want to pass this trial. Sliding can get you into trouble, so try light brake pressure and coasting to stay planted in the curves.

Lean in the direction of his vehicle if he starts sneaking by and try to cut him off. Don't leave him enough room to pass next to you and he'll have to fall back.

Overtake 2
Track: Piazza della Signoria 2, Florence • Car: Noble M12 GTO3

Car #7: Lap 1, 3:01 remaining
Car #6: Lap 1, 2:44 remaining

Car #5: Lap 1, 2:22 remaining
Car #4: Lap 2, 2:07 remaining

Car #3: Lap 2, 1:29 remaining

Car #2: Lap 3, :39 remaining
Car #1: Lap 4, :03 remaining

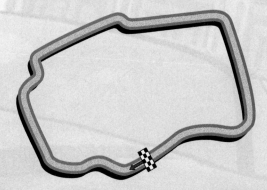

 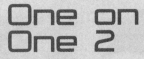

One on One 2
Track: Northern, Stockholm
Car: Noble M12 GTO3
This is a quick one-lapper; just hold the lead. Pull in front of the Porsche and cut across the first corner to block him from passing.

Timed Run 2

Track: Piazza della Signoria 1, Florence
Car: Noble M12 GTO3

Nighttime in Florence is bad for driving, but learn where the harsh turns are and plan ahead for them. Start your turn early and slide through it with the Noble.

The toughest part is in the southeast corner. Several sharp turns make up this "W" shape, and you can't build much speed between them. Get as wide as you can on the entrance to cut through them more cleanly.

Hot Lap 5

Track: Duomo 2, Florence
Car: Noble M12 GTO3

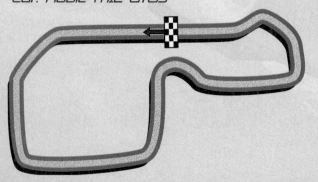

Ah, an old favorite. This is one quick lap around the first track you ever raced on the Kudos World Series, the Duomo 2. Keep to the absolute inside of the curves and use the tire treads on the ground to show you the best path. Look to hit 17 seconds in the part of the track just south of the finish line and you'll make it in time.

Street Race 3

Track: Battistero 1, Florence
Car: Noble M12 GTO3

This time, instead of going inside, take the outside of the first turn. Slide out from the last position and up around the right side of the Porsche. The cars leave an alley on the right that you can scoot down to get into second place.

Stay in third and follow the leaders down through the second light curve. Continue your pursuit on the left side of the track toward the next turn.

This guy is driving your car, so you have to draft behind him to overtake. Do so and you'll have a better vantage point for the first turn. You also can try to push him into the wall to see if he'll wipe out, but don't lose control in the process. From there on out, it's an easy race with lots of wide turns.

Floor it down the stretch and just catch the back of the lead car (he's coming across the lane) with your nose as you brake to spin left. You just barely throw him off, but the second-place car flies in and knock him off course. This gives you a chance to recover and run down the line, though you'll probably get paced by your two friends.

Speed Camera
Track: Nordschleife 12, Nürburgring
Car: Noble M12 GT03

No worries; you're set up on the inside of the next turn and can cut the other two cars off to keep your first-place position for the rest of the race.

One on One 3

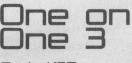

Track: KGB Corner, Moscow
Car: Noble M12 GT03

Get up to about 90 as you pass the blue signs on the side of the road. You're approaching the famous Karussell—a banked turn of concrete that resides on this real-life Nordschleife track. Get down along the wall of it doing about 75 to grip it and ride

One last lap down a Nürburgring track completes this series. Draft behind the Ferrari until you have enough speed to cut out and move ahead a few cars. You want to be behind the Porsche (in fourth place or better) after the right turn, then take third place by the time you hit the blue signs.

When you get halfway around, hit the gas and accelerate all the way until the embankment ends. Merge back with the normal road here and stay on the gas all the way to the gate to hit 130 mph.

Street Race 4

Track: Nordschleife 10, Nürburgring
Car: Noble M12 GTO3

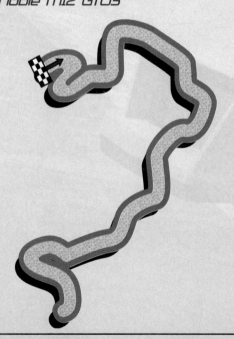

At the top of the hill, get down into the banked turn behind the lead two cars and keep your speed at around 75 mph to stay on the wall. Take it all the way to the end and you easily pass the other two, which

got off a little early. Stay on the track at a decent speed for the rest of the course (no lawn jobs) and they'll have a tough time passing you.

EXTREME SERIES

The cars keep getting more amazing, and the tracks keep getting tougher. This series is full of Street Races, so this section will help you get the early lead.

Recommended Cars:
At this later stage of the game, you'll be able to pick out a car that best matches the driving style you've adopted. Here are a few of the best:

Ferrari F50
The F50 is the best car on this track when you need to get the job done, but take some time to learn how to drive well if you're not used to their speed and tight handling. Use the Ferrari F40 as an alternate vehicle.

Jaguar XJ220
On the other end of the spectrum, the Jaguar is a great power slider. It's also got excellent top speed and acceleration that can put you in the lead for Street Races and One on One trials.

Ascari KZ1
The most capable car in the series isn't necessarily geared for all the tight turns in some of these races, so make it a second or third purchase that can help out if you're struggling.

Porsche GT2
On the tighter tracks that don't require top speed, the GT2 handles better than the Jag or the Ascari, so consider it for a backup vehicle.

ahead of time. In the first curve, for example, brake short to cut close to the inside. Emerge on the right side and recover, but you have to move left to make the next right turn, so don't accelerate to full speed yet.

Dealing with the bridge crossings is the tough part. Read your map to see what turn is approaching so you don't have to rely on your eyes in the dark, and think of each small west-east stretch as a single turn. Take them both in one wide motion. It doesn't require much braking to get the perfect line and extra speed.

Overtake
Track: In the Loop, Chicago
Car: Jaguar XJ220
In the Windy city at night (again). It's especially tough to overtake these quick competitors. Here are a few tips to help you get through.

After the first corner, there's a huge divider in the road, so stay out of the middle to avoid it. Dive left to get an easy setup on the outside of the upcoming right-hand turn.

Timed Run 1

Track: River Crossing, Chicago
Car: Jaguar XJ220
Keeping your lap time down in an course with so many turns is tough, but set up for your turns by reading them

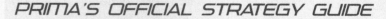

There's a hairpin on the western point that's very difficult to read in the dark. As you approach the point, drop your speed coming into the turn and stay left to make room for a light slide. With Jaguar's slippery tendencies, you should be able to skid around this bend pretty well.

Stay in control and come out of this turn behind the leader. You need to be only three or four lengths behind now, because it's time for the ol' smash-and-go. If you are close enough to draft, do so. Otherwise, move to

the left and run hard down the stretch. When he cuts out to take the turn wide, go inside and meet him with a glancing blow. He goes right, you go left, and the lead is yours after you recover.

Finally, look to passing your competition in the turns for an added edge. You can usually preserve the majority of your momentum and speed by letting a car on the outside absorb your drift. Think of it like a hockey puck riding the wall of an ice rin–just slide to the inside and let your opponent's fender be your guide.

One on One 1

Track: Lower Wacker Run, Chicago
Car: Porsche 911 GT2

Street Race 1

Track: Chicago River Tour, Chicago
Car: Porsche 911 GT2

Pick the Porsche for this trial because you'll be racing against a Porsche 959. You can match his raw stats and out-drive him. As you come out of the start, it looks as if your opponent is moving aside and letting you through.

But he's actually setting up a line so he can zoom by you in the next turn. Don't let him–cover up as much of the inside of the second turn as you can. Take it about half a car's width away from the inside rail

Come around on the outside of this turn to avoid the pack and stay to the right of the cars as you break lightly to stay in line. This puts you on the inside of the next turn.

and your rival either can't pass or he'll try and get thrown off course. Either way, the lead opens up to you.

Guard the turns so the eager opposition can't get a good look at a pass. If he slips by, stay close. You get an opportunity to draft and overtake before long if you can't do it in a turn.

One on One 2

Track: West on Wacker, Chicago
Car: Jaguar XJ220

Mimic your rival by picking the Jaguar. You can use the Porsche as well, but taking the Jag makes for a more even match-up.

Draft behind out of the gate until you can pass the leader on the right. This puts you inside for the next turn, so let your rival run into you and push you that way if he wants to. Otherwise, steer into first place.

If you're getting passed or feeling feisty, put your opponent into the wall for a huge lead. This track is only a single lap and you don't need much to win, but it's extra insurance.

One on One 3

Track: The Miracle Mile, Chicago
Car: Jaguar XJ220

Here's another easy single-lapper. Take the Jag or the Porsche, but either way, draft behind the Ferrari and move inside the first turn to cut him out of the lead.

As you pass, nudge your rival into the guardrail for extra insurance.

PRIMA'S OFFICIAL STRATEGY GUIDE

Timed Run 2

Track: Square Dancin'; Washington, D.C.
Car: Jaguar XJ220

You need to use a high-speed car here (like the Jaguar or the Ascari) to make the time. If you remember this track from previous races, you know you want to hit your top speeds in the straightaways on either side of the course.

Look to the two tight corners on the western side of the course as the places to make your time. Practice making conservative turns that practically wrap you around the inside guardrail. When you feel comfortable with them, work up to the highest speed that allows you to drive over the tire treads in the road and maintain a good race line.

Cone Challenge

Track: Capitol Thrill; Washington, D.C.
Car: Porsche 911 GT2

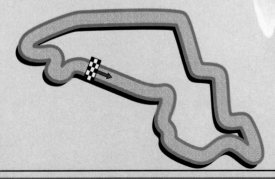

Take two laps through the gates and get that combo built up. The Porsche does a good job because it's so tight, but for Cone Challenges, whatever you drive best is going to work best.

Hot Lap

Track: Capitol Thrill 2;
Washington, D.C.
Car: Porsche 911 GT2

Follow the race lines in the road (the tire marks) to get this lap time nailed. The Porsche helps you control sliding better than most other cars.

One thing to look out for is a small bump or hill before the first turn. Take it on an angle or work around it to avoid an awkward landing and disruption of your critical line.

Street Race 2

Track: Northside Slide;
Washington, D.C.
Car: Jaguar XJ220

Barring a huge accident or other screw-up, you have to chase down the lead. Get a good position in the line from the start. Shoot for at least fourth place.

Stay with the pack and watch for opportunities to pass. If someone takes a poor turn, scrapes a wall, or slows, capitalize on it. The best place to pass is in the tight turn at the eastern point. You have four laps to get to first place, so stay focused and persistent.

Street Race 3

Track: Up and Over; Washington, D.C.
Car: Jaguar XJ220

Get up a good head of steam and charge toward the first curve. Pass the number six car on his left and ram straight into the number five (it is a Porsche).

The Porsche is in line to turn with everyone else, so your stunt creates chaos. Fortunately, you escape unscathed and can zoom to the front to take the lead.

You may have to try this a few times to get it to work. You might not generate enough force to disturb the line one time, and another you might make too much of a ruckus to pull away from. The opposition behaves differently every time you play, so be patient. Or invent your own wild overtake; you can even try to milk some Kudos from it!

Street Race 4

Track: The Tour; Washington, D.C.
Car: Jaguar XJ220

It's all about strategic driving this time. Draft behind the Porsche to your right toward the turn. When you enter it, though, cut left and weave through the traffic. These cars behave differently every time, but get the best position you can and don't worry about the lead yet.

This one's easy. Drive up behind the Ferrari ahead and follow him toward the curve. When he slows to take it, poke his rear passenger-side bumper and drive him into the opposite girder. If you do it right, he spears it head-on. If you don't catch this corner, he spins out in time and overtakes you as you struggle to regain control.

File off cars ahead while you're on top of them. If you can pick off the number three or four car and take his spot, you will be in good shape to overtake the front two or three one at a time.

If you nailed him well, your friend will be recovering until next Tuesday while you get a jump on the two-lap track. All's fair when 5,000 Kudos are on the line.

Speed Camera

Track: Speed Camera Track 2, Barcelona
Car: Jaguar XJ220

Street Race 5

Track: Yokohama Bay Tour, Yokohama
Car: Jaguar XJ220

Follow the race line laid out in the pavement for the lead-in turns. Get your speed up as fast as you can go without hitting the wall or sliding significantly as you stretch wide to take the final curve. Accelerate into it and watch that you're not skidding. You want smooth acceleration all the way through.

You've got to play this one like a master, but it's possible to win if you're up to the challenge. Draft behind the Porsche or any other trailing cars when you start until you pass them up. Move out to the left so you're pointed toward the turn's inside. You should hit at least 150 mph.

One on One 4

Track: Barri Gotic, Barcelona
Car: Jaguar XJ220

The three lead cars need to be lined up just right for this to work, but if you retry the race five or six times and hit them the same way each time, you'll get it.

Aim for the third car with your path ending up at the second. You bounce off the third, into the second, and graze the first, which funnels you onto the road in a perfect first-place position.

Even if you need to straighten out a little, you should be able to hold first here. It beats trying to fight these guys for it later.

Street Race 6
Track: Seaside Loop, Yokohama
Car: Jaguar XJ220

The rain makes things extra messy when the pack of cars piles up during the first turn. Run headlong into the pack. Get up behind the car in front of you and drive him toward the inside, wedging him between the wall and the other cars.

He should break through and give you a look at third or fourth place coming out. But these leaders are slow from the start, so keep up with them and pass in the next turn. Lean on one of 'em to help you through.

Watch your speed and traction in the heavy precipitation. You can slide through some of these turns, but keep it mild to stay under control.

Street Race 7
Track: Minato Mirai, Yokohama
Car: Jaguar XJ220

Accelerate to the corner and watch the cars stack up in front of you. Don't ram the pile, but skid toward the inside. There should be space for you to squeeze through into a strong third place.

Overtake the third-place car in the turn ahead, then follow the two leaders to the sharp, oval bend. You should be on top of them by now, so break through when they slow to make the turn.

The slow curves that make up the rest of this track prevent any major passing threat, so get to the finish safely to advance to the last series.

ULTIMATE SERIES

Here it is, the big finish. This series is loaded with good cars, so try them all to find your favorite. You're 19 courses away from completing the Kudos World Series!

Recommended Cars:
Enzo Ferrari
A little slow out of the blocks, but a real threat once it's moving. The Enzo will get you through the vast majority of this series.

Koenigsegg CC V8S
If you can say it, you can use it. It's worth owning, though not as versatile as the Enzo. It handles better on tight tracks and performs well in the Speed Camera event, though.

Street Race 1

Track: Nordschleife 7, Nürburgring
Car: Enzo Ferrari

The hardest part of this whole series is learning how to go from a wide-open track at 170 mph to a 70 mph turn. Knowing how and when to slow down comes with practice.

Slip between the trailing cars and cruise up behind the two leading vehicles. Since the Enzo is a late bloomer on acceleration, you will have to take these guys after the first mild turn. Be patient and you'll see yourself fly by in no time.

 Once you get the easy lead, you barely need to slow down over this track. The curves are gradual and the track is sprawling. It's a great practice for the series.

Street Race 2

Track: Nordschleife 8, Nürburgring
Car: Enzo Ferrari

Accelerate through the middle of the cars on either side and jockey for a third-place position entering the first curve. Stay behind the two leaders and follow them up to the banked turn.

Get down into the turn at around 100 mph and use the second-place car to keep yourself from drifting outward until you pass him. Stick to an easy pace of 75 mph as you follow the lead car out of the embankment and you will have sufficient speed to overtake in the upcoming stretch.

Street Race 3

Track: Nordschleife 9, Nürburgring
Car: Enzo Ferrari

Draft and overtake is the game plan here. Cut into fourth place in the first turn, and claw your way through the rankings by drafting off your opponents to build passing speed. The banked turn near the end is a great overtaking spot. Just watch out for the bump a third of the way through this track–too much speed here will send you into orbit.

Street Race 4

Track: Nordschleife 11, Nürburgring
Car: Enzo Ferrari

This is a long race that should be taken at a very calculating pace. You want to try and pass everyone, or at least the second-place car, by the midpoint. Stay on the gas all the way through the first part of the track until it's you and three lead cars out in front. You might get lucky and pass the third-place car here.

Into the first major turn, take advantage of your opposition slowing to jump up a place. If you do a little unorthodox grass riding on the inside here and set up a controlled collision, you can actually take the first-place car. But set your sights on at least a second-place position coming out of the turn with the leader's tail in direct view. You can take him in the next stretch by staying close and drafting.

Cone Challenge 1

Track: Uffizi, Florence
Car: Enzo Ferrari

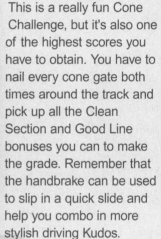

This is a really fun Cone Challenge, but it's also one of the highest scores you have to obtain. You have to nail every cone gate both times around the track and pick up all the Clean Section and Good Line bonuses you can to make the grade. Remember that the handbrake can be used to slip in a quick slide and help you combo in more stylish driving Kudos.

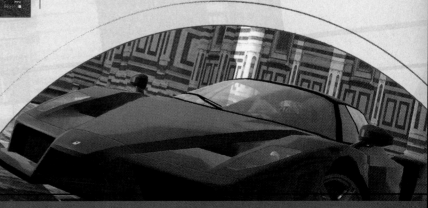

Street Race 5

Track: Battistero 1, Florence
Car: Enzo Ferrari

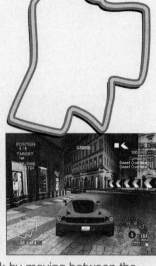

Sift through the starting pack by moving between the cars and into better position. Get into fourth place as you head into the left turn.

Look for a gap in-between the next two cars. They will either split and leave the middle open or veer to one side. It may be tight, but you should be able to find a clear spot to pass them both if you took the first turn strong and controlled. Now you're poised to go after the head car as you come up on the bridge.

An old technique gets you the lead if you're close enough to the head car. Line up on the left, graze him as you take the southwest corner turn near top speed, and veer off down the left alley with the lead.

Cone Challenge 2

Track: Northern 3, Stockholm
Car: Enzo Ferrari

You need to hit all your Good Line bonuses here if you want to clear this two-lap challenge. The Ferrari will respond if you guide it well, so have faith in its low center of gravity as you snake from gate to gate.

Just be extra careful with the 90-degree turns on this track. They seem pretty wide, but if you take them too hot you will end up in a wall. You should be able to slow to a  very safe speed and still accelerate out through the next set of gates to link them in time.

Street Race 6

Track: Speed Freak, Stockholm
Car: Enzo Ferrari

Accelerate past the slow cars in the back and follow the two leaders to the corkscrew. As they brake to take it wide, move in on the right and brake to take the inside at a leisurely pace. You overtake them and block their line through the turn.

You've driven here before, but remember your new car's strengths (better handling and acceleration) and limitations (lower slide potential and faster speed might mean you leave the ground and lose traction at times).

As everyone moves left out of the blocks, come to the right and use your speed to overtake the line going up the hill.

Overtake the second- and third-place cars in the first turn by deflecting off their side panels. This will put you within drafting distance of the leader, so stay on top of him. You will have a chance to overtake in the first couple turns of these concrete bridges.

Street Race 7

Track: St. Basil's Circle, Moscow
Car: Enzo Ferrari

Get up to speed and use the big, open turn ahead to overtake some opposition. Stay near the inside or center to avoid drifting out too far.

In pursuit of the lead, you fly downhill toward two archways. Make sure you're lined up to go through the one on the right before you leave the ground coming downhill. Jump out of control and you'll slam into something for sure. Otherwise, you overtake the leader and have a clean, open run to the finish line.

Street Race 8

Track: Cotton Tree Drive, Hong Kong
Car: Enzo Ferrari

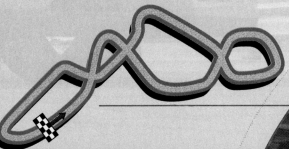

Street Race 9

Track: Yokohama Challenge, Yokohama
Car: Koenigsegg CC V8S
Overtaking for the lead is, once again, just a matter of being the first to enter a turn.

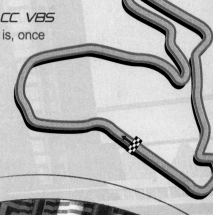

Use the Koenigsegg here for its amazing acceleration. Ignore the competition moving right as you head in to the first turn and hug the left side. As you enter the turn, you can engineer a controlled collision off the lead car (on your right) to glide neatly into the lead.

Throughout the four laps, the other Koenigsegg and some others on the track will be nipping at your heels. Watch your mirror and use your tail to deflect them away as they come up.

Cone Challenge 3

Track: *The Wharf, Sydney*
Car: *Enzo Ferrari*

This one's got a relatively low completion requirement on Expert level, but it's a short race. You have to do a lot of weaving and anticipating gate locations to win. On the cramped eastern point, stop-and-go driving usually works out okay. It gives you finer handling and promotes smaller slides that keep you in control but still add combo Kudos.

Street Race 10

Track: *The Rocks Route, Sydney*
Car: *Koenigsegg CC V8S*

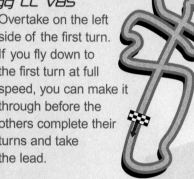

Overtake on the left side of the first turn. If you fly down to the first turn at full speed, you can make it through before the others complete their turns and take the lead.

Watch the abnormally tight hairpin turn in the middle of the western edge. Take it slow and tight—if you're passed, it has to be on the outside by someone taking a clumsier route that's slower on the exit. You can overtake again easily.

Cone Challenge 4

Track: *East Kinzie Crossover, Chicago*
Car: *Enzo Ferrari*

The last Cone Challenge is one of the more difficult ones simply because it's at night. The track layout is simple to learn, but you can't see some gates until you get up close, so it's hard to plan ahead. The darkness also obscures walls that are hard to avoid when they suddenly appear at the last second. Make a few practice passes to identify threats first.

Street Race 11

Track: East on Wacker, Chicago
Car: Koenigsegg CC V8S

Be patient in obtaining the lead here and your speed will win out in the end. Try to squeeze one or two extra positions out of the first turn by shooting through any available hole in the jumble of cars.

Gradually close the gap until your top speed and acceleration strengths boost you past the front two cars. This should take place about halfway through the first lap.

If you're leading now, take extra care in the southeast corner. This should take place before you make the turn in the northwest corner of the track, since these guys will match or beat your top speed in the straightaway.

Speed Camera

Track: Speed Camera Track 2, Washington D.C.
Car: Koenigsegg CC V8S

Don't bother accelerating through the first part of the track. Just get a nice position in the eastern point and back all the way up to the wall. Set up so you can see a straight line in front of you all the way to the final straightaway.

Launch from here and keep the gas down as you make mild steering changes to adjust to the road. You clear with ease in the Koenigsegg.

Street Race 12
Track: Catalan Challenge, Barcelona
Car: Koenigsegg CC V8S

Run hard on the left side into the turn. Before you turn the wheel, line up with the Porsche coming from your right so that your back end grazes his side as you make a hard turn. This re-stabilizes you in the corner and puts you on a good line to catch that leader.

Overtaking the lead car is a difficult process, especially in the long stretch ahead since your top speed is a little lower in this car. Try to play off your good acceleration in the tight turns ahead and make up for it[EM]you should be able to get right on top of him here. Otherwise, you can try the race with the Enzo for an earlier overtake if you're getting repeatedly stuck.

Street Race 13
Track: Grassmarket West, Edinburgh
Car: Koenigsegg CC V8S

Getting the lead here is a piece of cake. Pass the last cars and get into fourth without trouble. Stay to the right and keep the gas down. Meet the leader at the corner and you can edge him out of first place.

The rest of the race is mild if you've completed the others in this series, but this one is five laps long. Check the mirror frequently and guard your back to stay safe.

Street Race 14

Track: Nordschleife 1, Nürburgring
Car: Enzo Ferrari

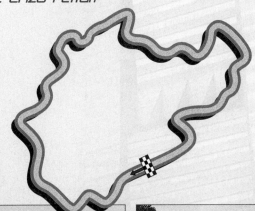

He's a quick one, but you can catch him at the first major curve. If you can't pass then, stay close and take a shot at it in the second turn (past the blue signs).

Whether you overtake or not, this course is a super-long one. It's somewhat of a rude awakening after all the shorter runs, so don't expect to nail it the first time. Take your time and practice for a few runs. It is your last trial in the Kudos World Series after all—why not make it last?

Draft the pack cars as they move forward. Mooch off one, then slide over to the next for more wind block-age. Before long you've passed everyone but the leader, who is about 40 lengths in front of you.

Bizarre Creations Ltd. Team

2D Art Lead
Gren Atherton

Audio Lead
Nick Wiswell

City Art Leads
Derek Chapman
Julie McGurren
Ben O'Sullivan
Mark Sharratt
Paul Spencer

Design Lead
Martyn Chudley

Programming Lead
Roger Perkins

Vehicle Handling Lead
Ged Talbot

Audio Content Lead
Mathias Grünwaldt
Rainer Heesch
Ian Livingstone—MTS

Audio Programming
Nick Bygrave
Keith Pickford

Car Art
Peter Moneypenny
Jonathan Reilly
Jeff Powell
Chris Wise
Game World 7 Ltd.

City Art
Alan Mealor
Gavin Bartlett
Boz Briers
Dianne Botham
Matthew J. Coward
Chris Davie
Eddie A. Draper
Paul Hesketh
Eddie Hilditch
Matthew Jeffs-Watts
Mike McTigue
Peter Roe
Joss Scouler

Design and Balance
Chris Pickford
Ged Talbot
Glyn Williams

Production
Peter Wallace
Brian Woodhouse
Allan Speed

Programming
Ed Clay
Paul Kerby
Phil Snape
David Worswick

Test
Barry Cheeseman
Simon Ellis
Peter Hall
Chris Speed

Live Test
Mark Craig

Tools Programming
Ian Wilson
Dave Al-Daini

Additional City Art
Lee Carter
Matt Cavanagh
Stuart Jackson
Steven Heaney
David McDonald
Alan Mullins
Phil Nightingale
Simon Pickard

Thanks
Gabor Soos
Mike Waterworth

Additional Programming
Stephen Cakebread
Sam Hall
Steve Penson

Bizarre IT
Stephen Gaffney
Andy Elliott

Bizarre Admin Support
Lisa Dutton

Bizarre Management
Martyn Chudley
Sarah Chudley
Michelle Langton
Walter Lynsdale
Brian Woodhouse

All our families and friends—too numerous to mention! All the guys and girls on our forums who've given us continual support and suggestions; Abbey Motorsport and Dynapack; Alexey Pajitnov; Andreas and Getaway Guys in Stockholm; Bill Chubb; David Stephen Jones; Dora Rogers; Gary Hall; Kats Sato; Keith Penny—Priory Practice Ltd.; Harvey Racing, Helen Caddock; Mike Clarke at HL Gorner TVR; James Jen; Kai and Yoshi at MSKK; Legal—Nik White at Brabners Chaffe Street; Ray Bucknell—Priory Financial Management.

Microsoft Team

Program Managers
Garrett Young
James Jen

Game Design Leads
Chris Novak
Bill Giese

Development Lead
Craig Cook

Art Leads
Kiki Wolfkill
Alex Hillman

Art
Jennie Chan
Franz Romer •

Art Content Coordination
LouAn Williams
Todd Van Horne •
Jennett Morgan •

Content Lead / Licensed Music Supervisor
Fred Northup, Jr.

Content Creation
Kiki McMillan
Michelle Lomba
Beth Demetrescu
Greg Collins •
Tyler Mays •

Audio Director
Andre Hoth (•/Anomaly Music Productions)

Audio
Greg Shaw
Joel Robinson
Ken Kato
Jerry Schroeder
Pete Comley
Mary Olson •
Tawm Perkowski (•/Weird Music)
Chris Vincent •
Justin Wood •
Mike Crank Imaging
Gordon Hempton of Soundtracker
DHM Music Design

Test Leads
Jeff Shea
Jimbo Pfeiffer

Test
Mike Yriondo
Joel Robinson
Mario Rodriguez
Gregory Murphy
Ty Balascio
Steve Dolan
Mark Medlock •
Chris Phillips •
Chris Beach •
James Sweet •
Matthew Kangas •
Scott Catlin •
Eric Johnson •
Bryan Sudderth •

Print Design
Chris Lassen
Jennie Chan

Product Managers
Scott Lee
Raja Subramoni

Associate Product Manager
Adam Kovach

User Testing Leads
Jerome Hagen
Eric Schuh

User Testing Assistants
Sylvia Olveda (Aditi)
John Hopson (Excell Data Corporation)

Localization Program Manager
Jenni Gant

Product Support
Craig Stum

Business Manager
Alfred Tan

Licensing Manager
Christian Phillips

Licensing
Kathy Kim
Mani Aliabadi •
Jim Hawk •
Andrew Lamb •
Frances King •/•
Denise Heimel •

Music Licensing
Lily Kohn
Bunmi Durowoju
Naomi Hopkins

Music Sourcing
Peter Davenport

Legal
Jama Cantrell
Hubert Cheng
Peter Becker
Mary Heuett
Pam Kilby
Sue Stickney
Judy Weston
Stacy Quan
Christine Spillers
TiAnna Jones

Senior Contract Specialist
Shari Davidson Maxwell

Contract Specialist
Rita Boyd

Contract Manager
Dennis Ries

•= Volt
•= ArtSource
•= Kelly Law Registry
•= S&T OnSite

Special Thanks: Ed Fries, Shane Kim, Phil Spencer, James Miller, Clinton Fowler, Andrew Walker, Jo Tyo, Matt Gradwohl, Matt Whiting, Ken Lobb, Norman Cheuk, Shannon Loftis, Chris Satchell, Josh Atkins, Howard Phillips, Matthew Lee Johnston, Greg B. Jones, Frank Pape, Todd Stevens, Jeremy Los, Boyd Morrison, Bill Fulton, Darren Steele, Chenelle Bremont, Stacie Scattergood, Jule Zuccotti, MS Studios; the localization teams in Dublin, Japan, Korea, and Taiwan. Thank you to all our Automotive Partners. See the in-game credits for the complete list of Project Gotham Racing 2 team members.

Fantasy leagues, meet video games.
Video games, meet fantasy leagues.

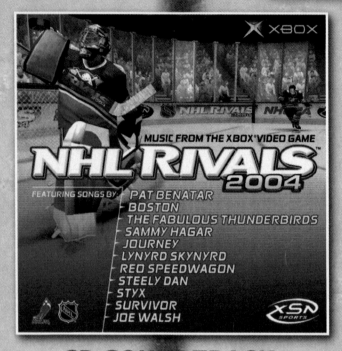